W9-BTC-344

EFFECTIVE
PARENTING
IN A
DEFECTIVE WORLD

effective parenting
in a defective world

how to raise kids

who stand out

from the

crowd

chip ingram

TYNDALE HOUSE PUBLISHERS, INC.

Carol Stream, Illinois

Visit Tyndale's exciting Web site at www.tyndale.com

TYNDALE and Tyndale's quill logo are registered trademarks of Tyndale House Publishers, Inc.

Focus on the Family is a registered trademark of Focus on the Family, Colorado Springs, Colorado.

Effective Parenting in a Defective World

Copyright © 2006 by Chip Ingram. All rights reserved.

Cover photo copyright © by Stockbyte/Veer. All rights reserved.

Author photo copyright © 2001 by Patrick Jagger. All rights reserved.

Designed by Jennifer Ghionzoli

Published in association with Yates & Yates (www.yates-yates.com)

Some of the "Putting It into Practice" exercises at the end of each chapter are adapted from the course workbook that accompanies the DVD series Effective Parenting in a Defective World (Atlanta: Walk Thru the Bible Ministries, 2003) by Chip Ingram. Used with permission.

Unless otherwise indicated, all Scripture quotations are taken from the Holy Bible, New International Version®. NIV®. Copyright © 1973, 1978, 1984 by International Bible Society. Used by permission of Zondervan. All rights reserved.

Scripture quotations marked NASB are taken from the New American Standard Bible, © 1960, 1962, 1963, 1968, 1971, 1972, 1973, 1975, 1977, 1995 by The Lockman Foundation. All rights reserved.

Scripture quotations marked NKJV™ taken from the New King James Version® copyright © 1982 by Thomas Nelson, Inc. Used by permission. All rights reserved.

Library of Congress Cataloging-in-Publication Data

Ingram, Chip, date.
 Effective parenting in a defective world / Chip Ingram.
   p. cm.
 ISBN-13: 978-1-4143-0383-3 (hc : alk. paper)
 ISBN-10: 1-4143-0383-1 (hc : alk. paper)
 ISBN-13: 978-1-4143-0384-0 (sc : alk. paper)
 ISBN-10: 1-4143-0384-X (sc : alk. paper)
 1. Parenting—Religious aspects—Christianity. 2. Child rearing—Religious aspects—Christianity. I. Title.
 BV4529.I54 2006
 248.8'45—dc22   2006013498

Printed in the United States of America

12 11 10 09 08 07 06
 7   6   5   4   3   2   1

DEDICATION

Theresa and I dedicate this book to our
four grown children, Eric, Jason, Ryan, and Annie.
Your lives have far exceeded our highest expectations
as parents. We thank God for each one of you and how
He has used you to teach us to parent. We love you
and enjoy being not only your parents,
but your adult friends.

CONTENTS

ACKNOWLEDGMENTS

Where do you start when a project that you've been working on (largely without knowing it) has been in the works most of your life? Thanks, Mom and Dad, for loving me, setting clear boundaries, eating breakfast and dinner as a family growing up, confronting me when I disobeyed, and forgiving me afterward.

Thank you, Theresa, for working together with me all these years to learn how, as first-generation Christians, to parent our kids.

Thank you, Eric, Jason, Ryan, and Annie, for allowing me to tell all those stories about our family that helped others grow, but had to make you a little uncomfortable.

Thank you, Curtis and Sealy Yates, Jan Long Harris of Tyndale, and Focus on the Family for believing in this project and making it a reality.

Thank you, Chris Tiegreen, for your partnership, insight, and for editing this teaching series in a way that resonates as much on paper as when taught to parents around the country.

And finally, thank you, Norrine Terrey, for helping all of us coordinate this project and protecting my time and energy so it actually was completed.

Most of all I thank God for His incredible love and grace given to me through His Word, myriads of people, books, tapes, counsel, reproof, encouragement, and modeling, which have shaped my thinking, my life, my parenting, and of course, my children.

INTRODUCTION

Tyler was like most of the other fifteen-year-olds who attended our church. He came from a good, solid family—his parents loved God and were doing their best to raise their children. Like everyone, they had their struggles, but nothing particularly unusual. So you can imagine my shock when I received a phone call informing me that Tyler had died. Not only was the suddenness of his death shocking, so was the cause. He had overdosed on heroin.

When we began to peel back the layers of Tyler's life over the next few days, I learned how a few bad decisions could destroy the life of a good kid. Long before, he had gotten mixed up in the wrong crowd and, in complete secrecy, had begun to do things his parents never would have imagined him doing. His parents eventually discovered that he had a drug problem, and they helped him through clinical rehab and biblical counseling. Everything seemed fine.

But one bad decision on one terrible night had devastating consequences. Tyler relapsed, and with one dose of bad heroin, he died in his room.

This is not the story of a kid from a bad family situation with negligent or abusive parents. This is the story of a middle-class American family—a mom and dad with good jobs who loved their bright, gifted son very much. This normal family suddenly found itself in a culture where a couple of mistakes can cost a kid his life. Tyler's parents realized they were raising their children in a very defective world.

At the funeral, I got a glimpse of the perverse subculture in which Tyler died. More than a hundred kids dressed in black and adorned with satanic emblems had found their way into our church. They were products of a twisted society, so completely turned around that they could hardly discern the difference between good and evil. They certainly weren't inhuman; in fact, one by one they got up and talked about how much they cared about Tyler and about how they didn't want to end up dead, their lives abruptly cut off like his by a drug overdose. Most of them were from what we would consider normal, middle-class families. Their parents, in many cases, were just as caring and well-intentioned as you and I are.

What was the problem? Why are so many loving parents shocked to find that their children's values come out so different from what they intended to teach them? The answer is that we live in a defective world, and good parenting can never "go with the flow" of the culture. That has always been true, but understanding it is perhaps more critical now than ever. Parents face enormous challenges today.

A Different World

When I was in school, we got in trouble for throwing snowballs at the school bus or for chewing gum in class. The kids who were *really* rebellious smoked, sometimes daring to do it in the school restrooms. Some would even smoke a little dope. Every once in a while, a girl would get pregnant and have to drop out of school. There were plenty of opportunities for trouble, but those opportunities pale in comparison to today's.

Now the stakes are higher. It's possible for your children to make one wrong decision and be HIV positive. Or they can be unwise for a moment, get in the wrong car, and end up at a rave. They have almost unlimited options for getting involved in drugs. Your daughter can even take a drug without knowing it, unaware that the guy she's with added a little something to her drink, and be raped while she sleeps it off. Or your children can go to school one day and come home forever traumatized from witnessing some of their best friends getting shot in the hallways. Life as a kid isn't what it used to be.

Imagine falling asleep forty years ago while watching TV in your living room. When you dozed off, you were watching a sitcom about a normal, traditional family, the kind with a dad and a mom and two or three kids. When you wake up this year, the TV's still on, but the normal family in the sitcom has one parent and children from two or three different marriages, or it has two parents of the same gender—and in either case, the children seem to be more "together" than the parents. Most kids growing up today don't have a clue what a normal family is, and the average parent doesn't either. Somewhere in the last few decades, we went from Ozzie and Harriet to Ozzy Osbourne, from Beaver and Wally to Beavis and Butt-head. As the stakes have gotten higher, principles of parenting have gotten more difficult to uphold—and more neglected.

We need to understand the kind of world our children are living in. Many of your children's friends have never been taught the difference between right and wrong because their parents either don't know it or are too intimidated by the culture to insist on it. Responsibility has given way to relativity, and moral chaos is the result. The world has changed; it's uncertain, it's violent, it's fearful, and it's defective.

It takes incredible wisdom and discipline to help your children navigate through the land mines of change, moral relativism, information overload, drugs, alcohol, peer pressure, and sexual immorality. It's even more challenging to keep them focused on living in a way that pleases Christ. Is it really possible for your children to grow up in all this mess and be godly, pure, responsible young adults? Can you be an effective parent in a defective world? Is there hope?

The answer is an emphatic "Yes!" There's hope. God has a plan.

We have a book, in fact, that is filled with stories of cultures more vile and evil than the world we live in today. In the midst of cultures in which ritual infanticide, religious orgies, perversities like incest and bestiality, and rampant occultism were quite common, God raised up godly children like Joseph and Moses and Daniel. He even chose to enter the womb of a godly teenage girl growing up in a pagan empire, making her young motherhood the humble means through which He would visit our fallen planet. All of these young people revolutionized the future. Depraved environments never prohibit God from accomplishing His purposes through children of righteousness. He can take ordinary parents like you and me and, with His Word and the power of the Holy Spirit, teach us to help our children break through the culture and even transform it.

Parenting by Grace

If you think our children's crises are only reflected in extreme situations like Tyler's, let me assure you that they can show up in anyone's home—even mine. Parenting today is tough and often confusing. I know that from personal experience. As a teen, one of my sons went through about four years of rebellion. By God's grace, he didn't cross any boundaries that left enduring scars or irrevocable consequences on his life. At times he'd miss dinner for a wrestling practice; while I felt really guilty about this, I was incredibly relieved that he wasn't there. The level of tension and conflict when he was around was so high it was painful. We were constantly at odds, pushing each other's buttons, making each other crazy and angry. He was (and still is) a very intelligent kid, so he knew exactly which buttons to push. He'd get right up to my limit, then back away before I exploded. We drove each other nuts.

To be honest, I did a lot of things that, in retrospect, didn't help him very much. We lived with unresolved conflict for years because neither he nor I really knew how to resolve the conflict. He got to the point of telling me that while I was an okay person, he wished I hadn't been a Christian because he wasn't sure he could buy any of this stuff about Jesus. As a pastor, that put a dagger through my heart. He could not have hurt me any deeper.

Even in the midst of our conflict, my love for my son was never broken. Love was what held it together when nothing else did. Through it all, God worked greatly in him and me, and he did a complete, dramatic 180-degree turn. Today he is a Christian songwriter and worship leader.

My son's mom, Theresa, and I married when he and his twin brother were a little over four years old. The boys never knew their biological father, and I was privileged to adopt them two years after our marriage. But all the baggage and struggles that you can imagine have been a part of our journey. It took years, not months, for some deep connections to occur. Along the way, Theresa and I were blessed with two additional children, a girl and a boy.

On top of the challenges that come from living in a blended family, our family ministered for more than twelve of our kids' most formative years in Santa Cruz, California, an ultraliberal, anti-Christian community in which the culture and public schools held beliefs that were 180 degrees from our own.

I don't know what unique challenges your family faces. But whether or not you're part of a blended family, you have to be prepared to help your children navigate some of the same potentially treacherous situations that Theresa and I did.

Will we fail sometimes? Of course. I hope I never give you the impression that it has all been smooth sailing for Theresa and me. We went through seasons of rebellion and times when we sat up in bed and cried in frustration because we had no idea what to do in this parenting journey—just like many of you have. I've been so mad at times that I've had to stay in the bedroom before I could talk to one of my kids, afraid that I might say something I'd forever regret if I didn't. There are times when you'll get discouraged and become convinced that your children are never going to change, but don't give up. Raising children is a learning process, and no parent is going to get it all right. We can, however, glean some powerful, timeless principles from God's Word to help us equip our children for the world they live in.

What I want you to know is that the pages that follow are not theory or pie-in-the-sky speculations of a never-had-a-problem pastor and his wife. This book is written from the grace-given experiences of a single mom who married a young, naive, would-be pastor, and both of them are first-generation Christians. It includes some of the lessons we've learned—both from personal experience and from years of pastoral counseling, psychological research, and Bible study—about bringing up confident, Christ-centered kids in a culture that is at odds with scriptural priorities. Specifically, the book discusses how to

- model right living and priorities
- build strong bonds with your children
- affirm your children's significance and security
- teach the importance of obedience
- use discipline lovingly and effectively
- persevere through mistakes and tough times

- pass on five key life lessons to help your children thrive in our culture

Because we as parents sometimes act based on cultural cues and pressures we don't even recognize, the book also looks at some parenting myths that run rampant in our culture and compares them to what Scripture has to say. Finally, each chapter ends with a section called "Putting It into Practice," which lists a number of exercises and questions you can use to immediately apply the principles and practical ideas in your family life.

A Word of Hope for Single-Parent and Blended Families

For many, picking up this book is a last-ditch effort. You're discouraged and frustrated. You have children from two different marriages and possibly some out of your present union. Or, you are walking alone with the children you once parented in partnership with someone you loved. Almost all the Christian books and talks on parenting seem to come from the ideal biblical family perspective of one man, one woman, and the children from their union. They can make you feel as if you've missed your chance to raise good kids.

Unfortunately, it's a fallen world, and the breakdown of the family has not left Christians untouched. Maybe you, like my wife, Theresa, came to Christ after being abandoned by your mate. Perhaps you came to Christ after a nasty divorce, or maybe you read these words with sadness and heaviness of heart because you and your spouse were born-again Christians who never dreamed divorce could touch your life. But the reality is that, for whatever reason, many reading this book are either single parents (like Theresa was) or are in a blended family with challenges that most people simply can't comprehend.

I want to end my introduction with this encouragement: If God allowed Theresa and me to end up with four wonderful, godly children when the odds were so stacked against us, He can do the same for you. No situation is beyond His grace, and no parenting task is too difficult for Him to walk you through. Wherever you are in the parenting journey, He's right there with you.

1 / How to Raise Positive Kids in a Negative World

A few years ago, the popular prime-time sitcom *Roseanne* featured a dysfunctional family. The mother, in spite of being hilarious, whined almost all the time. She and the father, in spite of having tender moments with one another, fought constantly. They dealt with complex issues without much of a moral compass, and they reared their children in survival mode, with almost no hint of a proactive agenda for them. Guess how their children turned out? Morally aimless, with early pregnancies and dysfunctional relationships, frequently in trouble at school, often hanging with the wrong crowd, experimenting with dangerous drugs, and seemingly destined for a series of broken marriages and dead-end jobs.

But as the show often pointed out, deep down this family loved each other. Plus they were good at one-liners. It was the typical American family, as defined by Hollywood.

I know that using a fictional family as a case study has some drawbacks, but the fact that this family resonated with middle

America is enlightening. Its portrayal had a lot of truth to it: Many parents live in survival mode while trying to raise basically good-hearted kids who, in spite of their life-shattering mistakes, really mean no harm. People watched this sitcom because they could relate. Its crude humor and dysfunctional relationships played out in prime time what was actually occurring in "real time" all over America. Here was a family in crisis who could laugh about it.

But what appears funny from afar is often devastating up close, and even Christian parents sometimes seem resigned to living from one crisis to the next. Many of us are afraid our kids are going to get into trouble, and every time they veer this way or that way, we go nuts from anxiety. So we create a lot of fences and walls around them, rules and provisions that will keep them restrained and keep us from having knots in our stomach at night. On top of that, we open as many positive gates in those fences and walls as we can— enrolling them in enriching extracurricular activities—hoping that our open doors will lead them into all the right places.

It's easy to look at contemporary culture and begin parenting out of fear. Scared of what might happen, many of us become preoccupied with what we *don't* want our children to do—"I don't want them to get hooked on drugs" or "I don't want them to suffer the consequences of illicit sex." That's fear, and it leads to a defensive, tentative, and often overprotective approach to life.

The result is that we can smother our children or insulate them, forbidding them from engaging in activities or associating with anything or anyone that could bring them harm. We are easily guided by the land mines we want them to avoid rather than the character we want them to develop. When we do that, we're always emphasizing the negative to them rather than the positive. Not only is that counterproductive, it requires more effort than we can give; if carried to the extreme, it demands our being with them everywhere they go. Also, it teaches them to depend on us to protect them from a world full of negatives, so they never learn the skill of living positively in dependence on God. Furthermore, when our desire to protect our children makes us mistrust them, they can be powerfully, negatively affected. Mistrust often becomes a self-fulfilling prophecy. Children begin to act in ways that validate our mistrust, and that gives us even more reason to be suspicious.

It's fruitless to parent either without direction or from a reactionary anxiety that tries to anticipate and avoid any danger our kids might face. Deep down we know this, and we crave direction and practical tools that will help us restore sanity to our lives and help our children grow into true maturity. As much as we might laugh about the eccentricities of our culture, most parents realize that the culture has shaped their children in negative ways. We need God's perspective on our kids.

> *We are easily guided by the land mines we want our kids to avoid rather than the character we want them to develop.*

Being a Father Himself, God has a lot to say about how to teach and care for children. Some of it is very general, the "big picture" perspective, and some of it is very specific. Before we get into particular tools and techniques for biblical parenting, there are four foundational principles that we have to understand first. We'll cover the first two principles in this chapter; principles 3 and 4 are explained in chapter 2.

Principle 1: Set Clear-Cut Objectives

Picture in your mind a target: a bull's-eye surrounded by concentric circles. That picture portrays the first important principle, a principle that will spare you years of aimless and indecisive parenting. It will keep you from being a passive or reactive parent and allow you to parent with purpose. Proactive parenting requires a target.

That's how effective parenting begins: with positive, clear-cut objectives. If you want to make a real difference in the lives of your children, you'll need to be firmly convinced of this principle. As they say, if you aim at nothing, you'll hit it every time. You can't really get on the road to effective parenting until you have some idea of where that road is going, of what kind of kids you want to end up with. Fear-based or go-with-the-flow parenting can be disastrous; the flow often goes in the wrong direction. Positive, clear-cut objectives will guide your decision making on the many occasions when decisions seem difficult to make. What are you trying to accomplish with your children? Do you have a clear target?

Be aware, however, that just as important as deciding to set a target is being careful to choose the right one. A man nearing retirement age was telling me that his son, a thirtysomething guy who had two failed marriages, still wasn't sure what career he wanted to pursue and had abandoned the family faith. This son lived a reasonably self-sufficient life and justified his lack of direction—aimlessness made him feel "free." I detected a high degree of disappointment in this father's voice; he clearly had an agenda for his son that had not been fulfilled (or perhaps an anti-agenda that *had* been fulfilled). None of his attempts to steer his son away from bad choices had been successful. But with a sigh of resignation, he looked at me and said, "At least he seems happy. I guess that's all a parent can hope for."

That's a false target. Our culture has deeply ingrained in us that the real goal of parenting is to raise happy children. That's a "Happy Meal" approach to parenting, and children are enthusiastic supporters of it—evidenced by the fact that kids choose 50 percent of a family's fast-food restaurant visits, according to one marketing group.[1]

And this keep-them-happy approach applies across the board. Because this philosophy is so ingrained in our society, we've bought into the lie that our children are deprived if they aren't involved in soccer, ballet, baseball, gymnastics, piano, and every other activity available out there—all while wearing the "in" kinds of clothes with the right labels—even when their demanding schedules keep us driving back and forth across town several times a day. It's really hard to resist this current of our culture; resistance requires an intentional and persistent effort, especially when your kids try to convince you that you're persecuting them by going against the grain. But if we don't, the culture, not God, will bear its own fruit in our kids.

Examine society's picture of parenthood carefully. It tries to convince us that the target of a good parent is to ensure their children have highly developed athletic prowess, refined social skills, and the best and most prestigious education, all of which should lead to greater upward mobility in life with greater opportunities and, of course, greater happiness. We can easily find ourselves bending over backward to make sure our kids never have a bad day and never lack any opportunity for success that might be out there. And the pressure's on, because if we fail at any of these points—if we don't work hard enough to earn enough money and rearrange our schedules to make enough time—we (and others) might feel as if we've done a bad job as parents.

I've got news for you. This is a dead-end street. The difference here is not simply a matter of parenting style, it's a matter of distinguishing between your dream for your child and God's dream for your child. Do you understand what you want to produce—or more importantly, what God wants for your kids? You have a tremendous opportunity to shape these vessels of the Holy Spirit and help them fulfill God's calling. God has a plan for your children that fits with His overarching purpose. What are you doing to set your children up for success as God defines it? You can't hit the target until you know what the target looks like.

PARENTING POSITIVELY

Fortunately, God gives the abridged version of His strategy for us as parents in Ephesians 6:4: "Fathers, do not exasperate your children." That's a negative command, but Paul then turns it around and states it positively: "Instead, bring them up in the training and instruction of the Lord." He warns against overcorrecting children, against placing demands on them that will be counterproductive. The idea is to create the conditions that make it as easy as possible for your kids to understand and embrace God's instructions and His ways.

Fathers especially get a little nudge in this passage. We'll explore the thought more deeply later, but for now, notice that God wants dads to have some real initiative in the family. Fathers are to take the lead in discipline and to implement it in such a way that children are better equipped to grow in faith. If there's no father in the household, it may take some creativity and initiative on your part for your children to be influenced by positive male role models—grandfathers, uncles, family friends, and men from church can help. But discipline can really only be implemented from within the home. Dads need to know how to do that.

On the flip side, parents who really care about the welfare of their kids—in other words, almost all of us—need to guard against our tendency to overcorrect. We can become so focused on external details of performance that we end up spending most of our time pointing out where our children need to improve. The result is kids who will become frustrated and rapidly lose heart.

As parents, we need to have a clear idea of what's most important. There are moral issues on which we have to be uncompromising, and there are matters of style. You may not like your teenage son's experiments with facial hair, but if he's trying drugs, focus your attention on the right issue. One, biblically speaking, is amoral; the other has life-threatening implications. As much as possible, focus on the essentials and give some latitude on the nonessentials. In other words, pick your battles. If you don't try to dominate in every small battle, you're much more likely to win the war.

The positive side of the command is to "bring them up" in Christian teaching and discipline. The Greek word for "bring them up" is interesting. In classical literature, this word meant to nurture or develop, and it focused primarily on physical development. The emphasis was on helping children grow big and strong. As the Greek language progressed, however, the word

Focus on the essentials and give some latitude on the nonessentials.

came to imply the total development of a child—not just physical, but intellectual, emotional, and spiritual. That was the connotation of the word when Paul used it in Ephesians; he's encouraging parents to do everything they can do to help their children reach their full potential.

It's important to instill in your kids the confidence that you believe in them; let them know you're counting on their character to help them navigate the land mines themselves. It's much more efficient and effective to teach your kids survival skills than to walk every step of the way with them to ensure their survival. Focus on the internal issues in training them rather than simply focusing on the external behaviors. If your children learn godly character, you won't always have to place godly restraints around them.

> *If your children learn godly character, you won't always have to place godly restraints around them.*

Did you realize God gave you that much responsibility? Parents have a lot of territory to cover. We are to bring up our children by constantly nurturing them toward maturity and by using the tools of Christian teaching and discipline. It's a grace-filled process designed to instill faith in the next generation—and to shape the world and the eternal Kingdom of God.

DEVELOPING SHARP FOCUS

Having a clear target is one thing. The ability to focus on it consistently is another. The key to parenting is to rivet your attention on the bull's-eye in sharp focus.

According to Romans 8:29, God's goal for all of us, including our children, is not to conform us to an ideal but to the image of His Son. Remember that target you pictured earlier in this chapter? The bull's-eye is actually a person: Jesus. Your goal and mine as parents is to help each one of our kids become like Jesus.

This goal has nothing to do with hairstyles and sandals. Neither is it simply about stuffing a bunch of memory verses into your children's heads, conforming to the culture of a certain denomination, or rigidly observing a daily quiet time. Our task is higher and more ambitious than that. In fact, it's supernatural, and it will require supernatural help. The point is for your children to be kind like Jesus, disciplined like Jesus, others-centered like Jesus, and holy and pure not because they have to, but because they love Jesus and want to be like Him. Establishing spiritual disciplines can be a handy tool sometimes, but the real goal is to cultivate the kind of love for the Lord that shapes the dreams and character of your child.

Parents must have a singular focus and a daily prayer: "Lord, will You help me cooperate with You so we can work together on this gift You've entrusted to me? Will You help me prepare this vessel to be filled with Your Spirit, so that in ten, twenty, thirty years this child loves and trusts You, knows Your grace, and has values and convictions that reflect Your heart?" If you ever wanted to know how to get an A as a parent, this is it.

Your children may go to Harvard, or they may not go to any college at all. They may have a lot of letters after their name or none at all. They may be really good at sports or ballet because that's exactly what God has designed them to do, or God may have created them to do things that will never fit with dreams you've had or footsteps you've already walked in. All of those things begin to fade in importance once you understand that your primary goal is to help your child know God and be like Him. That recalibrates your life, rearranges your schedule, and helps you sleep easier at night.

GOD'S DREAM FOR YOUR CHILDREN

God's dream for your children is that they be holy, not happy. Sounds like a depressing goal to have, doesn't it? Let me explain why it isn't. It's true that the word *holy* has some negative connotations, but only because people have abused it over the years. When the Bible talks about holiness, it does not mean being moralistic, always serious, looking down on everyone, or dressing in long robes and secluding oneself in a monastery. Biblical holiness is winsome and joyful. It means "set apart" to God and being filled with His pleasures and purposes.

Parenting Myth: Your goal is to make your kids happy.

Parenting Reality: Your goal is to make your kids holy— set apart for God.

Most people, however, think holiness and happiness are mutually exclusive. Nothing could be further from the truth! Nowhere in the Bible are holiness and happiness separated from each other. God is very much interested in your child's happiness, but His way to happiness is different from ours. His does not involve over-whelming our children with a smorgasbord of activity, clothing them in the most expensive labels, and anxiously guarding them from every potential evil. God's way to happiness is Christlikeness.

God's dream for your children is that they be holy, not happy.

How do we know? "Those God foreknew he also predestined to be conformed to the likeness of his Son" (Romans 8:29). That's the ultimate goal of God's parenting, it's supposed to be the ultimate goal of ours, and it's also the only way to ultimate joy. Our culture's focus on making kids happy is generally focused on short-term happiness, not eternity-long happiness. That kind of parenting usually produces children who are always striving for more and better, with happiness always just out of their reach because more and better is never enough. They are never content. But the by-product of holiness is joy. If our focus is on cultivating the character of God in our children, we'll be setting them up for the kind of happiness that comes from genuine, deep joy—both now and forever.

When you know positively where you want to take your kids, you won't spend all your time worrying and fretting and being afraid of all the things that might go wrong. The focus on what you want to accomplish will keep you from obsessing about what you want to avoid. Your target will give you a positive, not negative, approach.

Principle 2: Practice What You Preach

Jack wanted the best for his son, David, both materially and spiritually. He wanted David to have good, solid character traits and to have the skills to earn a good living. Jack was honest enough with himself to know that he'd made a lot of mistakes in life, so he always preached moderation and discipline to David. "Don't develop bad habits. Work hard and honestly. Marry a good woman and be faithful to her. Stay out of debt." The list went on and on, and it was good advice.

The problem was that Jack didn't live up to his own list. He had developed some bad habits that played out in front of his son: He was constantly in debt, he always exaggerated his hours—sometimes by a lot—when billing his clients, and besides cultivating a desire for David to walk a different path, he didn't seem to have learned much from his string of broken relationships. Jack had even gotten several speeding tickets while teaching David to drive, insisting all the while that David obey the laws of the road. Jack's words to David were always good advice from the right motivation, but they usually contradicted his own life.

Effective parenting requires that we practice what we preach. Children will not shape their lives by what we say. They are keen observers of attitudes and behaviors, and parents are their first and most important role models. Our instructions only sink in when kids see them backed up with a character and lifestyle that's consistent with our words. Simply put, parenting requires a lot of integrity.

Paul's ministry sometimes illustrated the role of a parent. As a spiritual father, he wrote caringly and firmly to the church at

Corinth. He had led many of the Corinthians to Christ, and he wasn't away from them for long before many of them began to get a little off track and problems began springing up in the church. So Paul, inspired by the always gentle yet firm Holy Spirit, wrote them these words: "I am not writing this to shame you, but to warn you, as my dear children. Even though you have ten thousand guardians in Christ, you do not have many fathers, for in Christ Jesus I became your father through the gospel. Therefore I urge you to imitate me" (1 Corinthians 4:14-16).

The tone of voice in this passage is that of a father who loves his children deeply and, while not wanting to embarrass them, earnestly wants them to be aware of the dangers they face. They have plenty of "guardians," people who will give them advice about how to live as Christians, but only one spiritual father. Notice what shape Paul's warning takes: "Imitate me."

That's parental integrity. Those words come from someone who practiced what he preached.

YOUR MODELING CAREER

Since the goal is for children to grow up to act, look, think, live, speak, and pray like Christ, the method is to be that example for them. Based on the foundation of a secure love relationship, Paul's words to the Corinthians were, essentially, "Pray the way I pray, give the way I give, live a holy life like I do, even though there are a lot of unholy temples around you promoting ritual sex and vulgar sacrifices." The rules and disciplines didn't need to be drilled into them; they needed to be exemplified. The Corinthians had a living model to observe. That's not a complicated curriculum.

The principle of modeling is that we cannot impart what we don't possess. Sometimes we think parenting consists of a to-do list; we feel like we need to do this, that, and whatever; give more time here; adjust the schedule there; then give the kids specific opportunities, experiences, and education. And while all of those things may flow out of our parenting, they aren't the essence of it.

The truth—and this is a really scary thought for all of us—is that your children are going to be a lot like you. For better or for worse, they will follow the patterns you set before them. That's why there are so many second-, third-, and fourth-generation addicts, abusers, criminals, and debtors. Negative traits are passed from generation to generation, cycle after cycle. The good news, though, is that positive traits are passed down that way too. You are the model in whose image your children will be shaped in their most formative years. So if you want your kids to be Christlike, what does that mean for you? Be Christlike. You need to be what you want them to become.

The old saying is really true: Children won't do what you say, they'll do what you do. Not only is that solidly biblical, it's basic psychology. A social psychologist named Albert Bandura did landmark research in this area, specifically on the issue of learned violence from media characters and other role models, and found that the most powerful educational tool on the planet is not a book, a speech, a video, a program, a seminar, or an online training module. It's modeling—providing an observable pattern of behavior—and doing it consistently.

That means that children who are exposed to violent images will tend to act them out. Children who are exposed to vulgar language will learn to speak it. Children who are exposed to bad money management are likely to mismanage their finances. Children who are abused are good candidates to be abusers one day. This is a frightening and solidly research-supported dynamic, but it's encouraging to know that it works in reverse as well.

Children exposed to positive, morally strong, responsible role models will tend to grow up as positive, morally strong, responsible adults. It's a golden opportunity for us to shape our kids. We can simply *be* the pattern we want them to follow.

MAKE IT REAL

Can you imagine lining your children up on the couch, looking them in the eye, and saying: "I want you to be like me. I want you to talk the way I talk, drive the way I drive, eat and drink the way I eat and drink, watch the kinds of shows I watch, handle your money like I handle my money, balance work and rest like I balance work and rest, and handle your anger like I handle mine"? Would you be comfortable giving them that kind of charge? If not, the most profound parenting decision you will ever make may be how you respond to what you just read.

Can you fathom the lifelong difference you could make in your children's lives if you stopped right now to identify the attributes that you're uncomfortable passing down to them and then systematically began to allow those attributes to be conformed to Christ? You must become who you want your children to become.

If a responsibility that heavy causes you to feel an enormous amount of pressure, let me encourage you. You don't have to be perfect. In fact, you couldn't pass perfection down to your kids if you wanted to; they're fallen human beings, just like you and me. What you *can* do, however, is demonstrate how godly people handle themselves when they blow it. Authenticity is the goal, not perfection. Let them see how you deal with failure as well as how you deal with success. You can demonstrate what it means to repent, to confess, to humbly accept responsibility for your mistakes, and to ask forgiveness. In fact, asking your child to forgive you for a mistake is one of the most powerful teaching tools you have. It's not about having it all together; it's about living out what you believe day by day and responding appropriately when you miss the mark. It's impossible for you to be perfect for your kids, but *anyone* can be authentic.

As I write this, one of my sons has a brand-new baby, my first grandchild. It's easy for us to think that there's not much a parent can do for a one-month-old, but even at that early age, my son can invest in his daughter's eternal future. The more passionately he follows Christ, the more godly that young lady is likely to become. The more he walks with Christ, the more his daughter is going to catch that relationship. The more he lives a transparent life before her, the more she will grow up to be humble and transparent. Character is always more caught than taught. Always.

When Jesus said that "everyone who is fully trained will be like his teacher" (Luke 6:40), He wasn't putting a heavy burden on people in teaching or parental roles. He was giving every parent and teacher an opportunity to nurture honest, genuine disciples. You can make tons of mistakes and still raise awesome kids by showing them how God has mercy toward you and gives you hope. When children see change in their parents, it gives them hope that their failures aren't final either. They grow up to be authentic human beings who are aware of their faults and who embrace God's grace.

Character is always more caught than taught. Always.

I can remember numerous times when I blew it in front of my kids. My tendency was to get frustrated when they didn't follow clearly laid-out instructions. My fuse could be short, and though my words to them in such cases were right, they were often delivered with an angry spirit. When I began to see the effect of my reaction on them, I was compelled to repent and apologize, affirming that what I had said was appropriate, but acknowledging that I had said it in the wrong way. Over time, I began to see them play out the same dynamic with their siblings; they would take the initiative to apologize for their offenses toward each other. Because I had shown them how I dealt with my failures, they began to imitate me in dealing with their own.

Ask yourself this question: "Do I want my children to turn out like me?" Can you honestly say that the way you live—your worship, your lifestyle, your prayers, your devotion, your habits, your stewardship, your generosity, your schedule, your love and kindness—is the way you want your children to live when they grow up? What we parents have to accept, whether we like it or not, is that there's nothing we can do to change this dynamic. It's as universal as gravity. Children are shaped by role models, and they always start with their parents.

If you find yourself telling your children to do a lot of things that you haven't learned to do yourself—such as get rid of a bad habit, control a quick temper, or be honest with others—you need to stop talking and start doing. Your words aren't going to mean very much if your life isn't backing them up.

Whenever I present this lesson to an audience, I see looks of despair on the faces in front of me. I know what this principle makes people think: *Man, if my kids handle their anger the way I do, they'll have major problems for the rest of their lives. If they drive the way I drive, half the city's in danger. What if it's too late? What if I've already modeled too many of the wrong things?*

Don't despair. God can take the most negative past and produce a positive future as we turn wholeheartedly to Him for help. As Scripture promises, "Love covers over a multitude of sins" (1 Peter 4:8). I can't tell you how many times I went to my children when they were small, got down at eye level with them, owned up to violating one of my own standards, and asked them to forgive me for the behavior I knew they'd just witnessed. My kids didn't learn how to be perfect from me, but they learned how to be real, and they learned it because they knew they would see me seeking to deal with my own issues with the same measures of grace and discipline I used with them. And although I'd love to leave you with the impression that I never have to do that anymore, it would be a lie. Even with my adult children, I find myself scheduling private time to own up to a careless word, a bad attitude, or some other personal failure that needs to be addressed.

Your parenting is about more than getting through the stages of development. It's an offering to God, a service to His Kingdom, and a stewardship of His precious gifts. It's also an offering to your children, a gift that will set them up for a fruitful life and an eternal relationship with their true Father.

For God and Children

As you begin thinking about how to parent effectively in a defective world, consider the two parenting principles outlined in this chapter: (1) Set clear-cut objectives and (2) Practice what you preach.

First, get crystal clear about your target. Remember that you are not called to produce successful, upwardly mobile, highly educated, athletically talented machines. (This may be a shock, but in all likelihood none of them are going pro anyway, okay? And even if they do, they'll most likely live the dysfunctional lives you see among the rest of the pros, and no parent really wants that for their child.) Giving your children great opportunities is good; it is not, however, the goal of parenting. Christlikeness is. Above all, seek to raise children who look and act a lot like Jesus.

Second, be what you want them to become. The greatest gift you can give them is not to teach them how to become Christlike. It's to be Christlike yourself. Love your spouse as your primary relationship in this world. Treat your children with both grace and discipline. Let love be the foundation of everything you do.

Ask yourself right now—and on a regular basis—*What needs to change in my life for my child's sake?* What relationship, addiction, habit, or attitude do you *not* want reproduced in your child? Pause and think about that.

Once you've identified a problem (or a list of them), ask God to help you deal with whatever needs to be dealt with. Meet with Him about it regularly. He's as interested in the character of your children as you are, and He is not reluctant to step in and help those who ask Him to. When you've asked Him for guidance and sought His answer diligently, begin to move forward in faith that He has answered. Keep your ears open, and He'll correct you if you get off base—you can count on that. But keep studying His Word, letting Him speak to you and following His lead. Together, you and He can come up with a game plan that will help you become exactly who you long to become, which will help your children become exactly who they long to become—for the glory of God and for the welfare of the next generation.

Putting It into Practice

In the space below, describe your personal target for successful parenting. However you define parenting success, describe it below. For example, "I want to teach my child one new character trait (such as obedience) every month, including memorizing a definition and acting out scenarios where the character trait is important in life," or "I will take Josh to the father/son retreat every year," or "Sarah will take care of her own laundry by age twelve and prepare one meal a month for our family starting at age fifteen."

LIST OF "WHATS"

Now try to give a "why" for each item you listed above. Example: If you wrote, "I will teach Jordan how to divide his allowance, giving a tenth to the church, saving a tenth for the future, and carefully stewarding the rest toward wise purchases," you might write, "My purpose is to teach Jordan how to be a good steward and to understand that everything belongs to God and is simply managed by us."

LIST OF "WHYS"

_____

_____

_____

_____

_____

_____

What are some positive ways your children model the example you have lived out in front of them?

_____

_____

_____

_____

What are some negative ways they model your example?

_____

_____

_____

What one positive step could you take this week to improve the way you model Christlikeness for your child?

_____

_____

_____

_____

2 / Building Relationships That Bond

When Todd started showing an interest in music, his parents were a little worried about the kind of music he was listening to. They were deeply concerned that his appetite for music would lead to values and relationships that would draw him away from Christ. They stood at a fork in the road; they could criticize his tastes and forbid his music from being played in the house, or they could guide him in his new interest. So they let him get a guitar, and as he learned to play, they began to tolerate his music. Then they began to *like* some of it. Todd's father added a drum set to the mix for his other son, Brad, and Dad himself joined in on bass. The three spent hours in basement jam sessions.

After Todd earned a reputation at school for being a good musician, he was asked if his band could play for the junior/senior prom. He accepted, and the entire band—including Dad—played for the high school dance. "I'm thankful that Dad joined in with us and became part of my brother's and my team," Todd later said, "rather than just criticizing from the sidelines." What could have been a family rift turned into a time of family bonding.

Parents often find themselves as adversaries to the very children they want to support. There are almost limitless issues that can potentially create a split between you and your kids. How can you demonstrate that you're on your children's team without compromising your principles?

Principle 3: Build Relationships That Bond

Parents, as we have discussed, should set a clear target and model the Christian life for their children. But that's not enough. Those two overarching principles must be lived out in a special environment, and that environment must be progressively characterized by love that is both genuine and expressed. When love isn't obvious in a parent-child relationship, that relationship weakens. And the more the relationship weakens, the weaker the parents' influence becomes.

Parents also must build relationships that bond. They need to make sure their children know without a shadow of a doubt that they are loved unconditionally. They must create an environment—through shared experiences, visible care and concern, and meaningful expressions of love—in which their own hearts become glued together with the hearts of their children.

Why is this important? Because there's virtually no limit to the number of factors that will try to pull you and your child apart. Peers can drive a wedge between you, and so can traumatic events, media influences, cultural trends and expectations, temptations, and so much more. The stronger your relationship with your child, the greater the probability he or she will embrace the values you hold most dear through the hard times.

The apostle Paul again provides practical instruction. "We were gentle among you, like a mother caring for her little children. We loved you so much that we were delighted to share with you not only the gospel of God but our lives as well, because you had become so dear to us" (1 Thessalonians 2:7-8). As with the Corinthians, Paul felt a parental responsibility toward the Thessalonians. And notice the language he uses to express that relationship: "we were gentle," "like a mother caring for her little children," "we loved you so much," "we were delighted," "you had become so dear to us." That's how he

There's virtually no limit to the number of factors that will try to pull you and your child apart.

depicts the maternal side of parenting. He wanted to love these Christians, these disciples, as a mother loves a baby.

That's the divine prescription for how a mother is to love a child—in intimacy and nurture. Not only did Paul and his colaborers share the gospel, they also shared their own lives with tenderness and care. Theresa would incorporate this maternal sense of nurture into every aspect of our children's lives. She would sing to them as she put them to bed, daily put them in her lap and read to them, and have deep conversations with them about what mattered to them. In their teen years, they would always go to her first with their deep emotional hurts—like the first time they got dumped by a boyfriend or girlfriend, or when they had their hearts set on making a team and got cut from the roster. Her years of nurturing brought them back to her whenever they were hurting. When you give your life to your child the way a mother does, the relationship deepens and connects.

The contrast in verses 11-12 complements the maternal role. "You know that we dealt with each of you as a father deals with his own children, encouraging, comforting and urging you to live lives worthy of God, who calls you into his kingdom and glory." That's the paternal side of parenting, according to Paul. This is how fathers love: encouraging, comforting, and urging. Dads help their children live lives worthy of their calling in a way that points toward the Kingdom and the glory of God. In other words, there's a target on the wall that looks like Jesus.

A word study on each of these fatherly words produces some interesting results. The word *encourage* applied to your children means you are their number one cheerleader. Fathers are good at yelling motivational and encouraging words at their kids' ball games. (I know, some get carried away and pressure their kids, but that's not the kind of coaching I'm talking about.) Those motivational cheers should also have some sort of expression in real life. That's a dad's role. When you see your children going through a tough time, you encourage them to keep pressing ahead. When you see them knock one out of the park, you give them a high five. Dads are to be their kids' biggest fans. You build relationships with your children when they know you're on their team. You tell them you love them, you encourage them to go for their goals, you let them know you have full confidence in them.

But it doesn't stop there. To comfort your children means more than most English translations of this verse can convey. That word *comfort* is sometimes translated as "exhort" or "admonish." It means to speak into the lives of your children words that will not only comfort them but also challenge them to be all God wants them to be. You provide them with the kind of security that makes them unafraid of failure—that's the comfort—and with the kind of accountability and drive that helps them reach the goal.

The third word Paul uses to describe a father's role is *urge*. It's a strong word, and it conveys the idea of a dad drawing a line in the sand and reminding his child of the consequences when that line is crossed. It isn't discipline for the sake of discipline; it's a statement that says, "I love you so much that I won't tolerate behavior that will be destructive to you."

Paul's picture of a father, then, is of a man who is on his children's side, who will affirm them whenever and however possible.

But when a dad sees a child begin to veer off track, he knows the child needs one of two things: correction or discipline. Correction says, "Honey, I don't feel good about this guy you're dating, and I don't think this is a good direction to go." Discipline says, "Honey, I told you I don't feel good about this guy, and we had an agreement. I'm holding you to it, and this is the way it has to be." It's gentle and comforting, but it's also firm and clear. It will give a child all the support he or she needs—in abundance. And it will zealously guard the boundaries that preserve his child's welfare.

> *Speak into the lives of your children words that will not only comfort them but also challenge them to be all God wants them to be.*

THREE IMPORTANT RELATIONAL AXIOMS

Three axioms will help motivate and encourage you to build a close relationship with your child. The first two express the same principle, one positively and the other negatively. The third will put the first two in perspective, especially in those times when you feel like you're fighting a losing battle.

Axiom 1: The *stronger* your relationship with your child, the *more likely* he will be to embrace your values and beliefs.
Axiom 2: The *weaker* your relationship with your child, the *less likely* he will be to embrace your values and beliefs.
Axiom 3: Tension, stress, and difficulties are normal.

As I've said before, you don't have the power to be a perfect parent who produces perfect children. You can take a lot of pressure off yourself if you get clear on that fact. You do, however, have the power to create an environment of love, truth, and grace that gives your children the greatest possibility to respond to God. Your kids are people who are going to make mistakes, especially as they grow into ages of greater responsibility and decision making. You can't prevent those mistakes, but you can set them up for the best possibility of success.

A word of warning, however: Don't approach parenting as a formula. As a pastor for more than twenty years, I've seen numerous people I thought were great parents—who loved God, modeled Jesus, and bonded with their children—have a child who went off the deep end. I've also seen the reverse dynamic. I know a girl who had an unbelievably bad background—her parents split up, her mother abandoned her, her father didn't want her either, and she ended up sleeping on a cot in the laundry room of someone else's house for three years during high school. And she's one of the most godly young women I've ever met in my life.

So there's not a one-to-one correlation where, if you push the right buttons, you get the right outcome—or, on the other hand, where you push the wrong buttons and it's a certain tragedy. You're important in your child's life, but you're not *that* important.

Don't approach parenting as a formula.

God is still sovereign; His purposes still allow for the unpredictable rebellion of human beings, and His grace still covers our failures.

The third axiom should help you relax. Every parent with toddlers, teenagers, or anything in between knows that stress is normal. The issue is not *if* your relationship with your child is going to be tested, but *when*. It will be. Your responsibility is to create that environment where you exhibit the kind of love that gives your child the best opportunity to respond to the grace of God. And then when you've given it your best shot and she still makes some bad decisions, you can let her bear the moral weight of her actions and trust that God is working in her life.

The bond you have with your children is like a bridge. All of those lifestyle characteristics they observe about you—the way you spend, how you manage your schedule, the words you use, the attitudes you present—affect them more positively when you have a deep relationship with them. Conversely, your modeling may affect them negatively when you haven't developed a strong bond. The tighter the relationship, the more easily beliefs and values are transferred into their hearts and minds.

It's also true that the stronger the bridge you make for them, the greater the weight of truth that bridge can hold. That's why the most important thing you can do, after walking with God yourself and getting a crystal clear focus in your parenting, is to create relational love in your home and spend time with your children. Then when the difficult times come, the superglue that holds you together will remind them that underneath the conflict, and behind the discipline, is love. They'll know they really matter to you and that you're on their side.

The tighter the relationship between you and your child, the more easily beliefs and values are transferred into their hearts and minds.

PARENT'S LIFESTYLE — values + beliefs — STRENGTH OF RELATIONSHIP — CHILD'S LIFESTYLE — values + beliefs

I know from experience both how challenging and how important this is. The one thing that kept our rebellious teen from walking away from our family was his conviction that we cared deeply for him. At times in the heart of the conflict, he'd say, "You know, I know you and Mom really love me." The relationship never became completely unglued because the foundation of it was love. I had decided long before that regardless of any problems I'd have with my kids, there was nothing they could do to stop me from loving them. Love creates boundaries like guardrails on a highway, but it never blocks the highway.

So how do you build relationships that bond? Let me share eight specific practices that will allow the Holy Spirit to build supernatural bonds between you and your child.

EIGHT ESSENTIAL KEYS

Every parent who's honest will admit to ups and downs like I had. There will be times when your tongue gets you in trouble, as mine often would, and times when you make decisions too quickly or not quickly enough. But as you strive to improve, you can minimize the damage of those difficult times by establishing a strong connection with your children. There are eight specific, practical things you can do to cultivate a bond with them:

1. *Unconditional love.* Years ago, a man who himself had been abused illustrated perfectly how not to express unconditional love to his children. He'd already had a couple of kids taken away from him because of his anger issues, and every time he got angry with the children still in his household, he'd threaten them: "You better straighten up right now, or I'll have you taken away like the other ones."

   Most of us are not that drastic, but we do have subtle ways of implying that we love our kids when they're good and don't when they're bad. Of course, we *do* love them unconditionally, but they interpret a lot of our words and actions as an expression of how much we love them. We have to be very careful. When we knowingly or unknowingly communicate that our love for them is based on their behavior, we're setting ourselves (and them) up for failure.

   When my son was going through his rebellious years, I'd take him out to breakfast regularly. I didn't necessarily want to be there, and I could tell he didn't really want to be there either—

he'd roll his eyes to make that very clear. Even though I didn't feel the emotions of love for him every moment, I chose to spend time with him to let him know that the love was there even when the relationship was strained. I constantly verbalized and affirmed that his mother and I both loved him very much. How did he respond? "Yeah, yeah, I know. Whatever." But I'd keep affirming it: "No, really, we love you, Son." I made it a point to separate my disapproval of his behavior (his actions and attitudes) from my approval of him—the person of infinite worth who would forever be my son. I couldn't see immediate results, but I saw them eventually. Unconditional love is a powerful relationship builder.

2. *Scheduled time.* I encourage parents, especially men, to keep all of their commitments on the same calendar rather than keeping separate ones at work and home. You may have a lot of important meetings with a lot of important people, but none of them are more important than your time with your kids. Get your family's names on your calendar or PDA too— breakfast, dinner, and recreation. Prioritize your time with the whole family, and when someone tells you that it's really important to meet with you at the same time you've scheduled time with your family, you can say, "I'd love to be there, but I'm already scheduled for another meeting. Can we do it another time?" It's amazingly effective. It works when we have two conflicting professional commitments, doesn't it? It can also work when our professional commitments conflict with our family commitments.

We think our family time is optional, that our spouses and kids will understand if we have to fit them in around the more urgent business of the day. But I've got news for you: Business deals will come and go, but kids are there for only a brief window of time and then they're gone. And what you do during that window makes all the difference in the world.

Contrary to popular belief, there's nothing wrong with putting fun family activities on your calendar. God has ordained them, and they belong there. Proverbs 17:22 says that "a cheerful heart is good medicine, but a crushed spirit dries up the bones." It's important for your family to maintain a "cheerful heart." Never fall for the lie that choosing the quality family stuff over the big projects at work is irresponsible. God usually looks at it the other way around.

3. *Focused attention.* Many kids get unfocused attention from us. Parents can carry on an entire conversation with their children while reading the paper or watching TV.

> *Never fall for the lie that choosing the quality family stuff over the big projects at work is irresponsible.*

"How was your day at school, honey?"

"Oh, it was great. Let me tell you . . . ," and then a story begins.

"Uh-huh . . . that's good . . . mm-hmm . . . oh, I see."

Or you ask about their day while you're driving, and as they answer, you find yourself trying to figure out whether you need to stop at the grocery store, or where you need to turn next, or if you should try to squeeze in an errand at the mall so you won't have to get back in the car later. Before you know it, the story is over and you hardly heard a word of it. Children are extremely perceptive observers of parental behavior. They know whether you're interested or not. And when you're not, it hurts. It weakens the bond between you.

Focused attention means that your body language says, "I'm interested," that your ears actually hear what's being said, and that you follow up with questions relevant enough to indicate that the conversation has some real value to you.

Our work or outside activities can easily pull us away from our families. Early in my life as a pastor and a workaholic, the phone would ring at home and I'd jump up and answer it. Frequently, there was a legitimate need on the other end of the line, and I'd do whatever I could to meet it. My wife would say, "Can't you just lighten up a little bit?" And I'd always respond with, "They really need me. I'm their pastor, and if I don't do this, who will?" You see, behind workaholism is a somewhat egocentric attitude that says, *I'm indispensable.* We think we're so important that everyone needs us—and no one else but us—to meet a particular need.

Most people who are too busy for their families, as I was, are too important in their own eyes. They don't realize that their importance to their family is more fundamental, in God's eyes, than their importance in their work. God's Word makes that clear in the way it prioritizes responsibilities for us. In both Ephesians and Colossians, for example, Paul follows his description of a Spirit-led Christian life with specific instructions in this order: our relationship with God, our relationship with our spouse, our relationship with our children, and our responsibilities in work and ministry. It seems clear that God's priorities for us follow that progression. Family time is important. One of the best ways to protect it is to get eyeball-to-eyeball with your children and talk with them like they matter—because they do.

4. *Eye contact.* This goes hand in hand with focusing your attention on your children, but it's the best way to make your attention obvious. Eye contact tells your child that he's important and you're listening.

I remember as a psychology major studying the effects of looking people in the eye and giving them focused attention while they talk. Eye contact is universally recognized as one of the

most powerful ways to communicate your interest in whomever
is speaking to you. With people close to you, it communicates

Eye contact tells your
child that he's important
and you're listening.

that you love them. And when children are
small, getting down on one knee to establish that eye contact speaks volumes to
them, even at their young ages.

5. *Maintain ongoing communication.* It will seem like I'm repeating
myself on this point, but there's a reason for the repetition.
There's a difference between establishing good communication
and maintaining it over time. A lot can happen to create
emotional distance between you and your children, and only
consistency over the long haul can protect against that. That
said, here are three ways to develop and maintain communication with your kids:

(1) Eat dinner together. Turn off the TV, sit down at the table at
the same time, and talk. Focus your attention so that you actually listen to one another and convey the attitude that whatever
your children say matters. I realize that's not going to be possible
every single night, but it should happen more often than not.
Dinnertime may be one of the most powerful opportunities to
build relationships that bond.

I understand that for many American families, dinner
together is in the minivan at the drive-through on the way to
the third practice of the week. That's understandable on occa-
sion, but there's a problem with it as a regular practice. I've
heard parents say, "I've never missed one of my daughter's
soccer games in four years." Though the motive to support
your child is admirable, I don't think there's a better way to
convince her that your entire family life revolves around her
and soccer. Play that out for fifteen years, and you'll have a

daughter who finds it very difficult to adjust to a world and relationships that aren't all about her.

Yes, it's very important to go to your children's activities and support them. It's dangerous, however, to center your entire lives on those activities. It's better to say, "We eat as a family at this time, and our family is what matters." Normally you can schedule around activities if you aren't attempting too many in one season, but occasionally you may miss a practice or two. Family is more important than soccer practice.

At that point, your child is likely to point out how much the coach is depending on her, and how her friends are going to start more games because they've been there every time. That's okay. The priority of family over what happens with nine-year-olds kicking balls around a field to get little trophies no one can find a year from now is self-evident. As an athlete who played basketball and baseball in college and coached in youth leagues, I love sports. But the whole organized sports experience is often out of balance and overrated. Twenty years from now, throwing the ball with your child in the backyard will have had much more lasting impact than putting them on a team while screaming parents put unbelievable pressure on their children to win a trophy.

Don't get me wrong. I'm *not* saying youth sports leagues are bad. I'm just saying that we easily get them out of proportion to the rest of our lives. They can easily become the center of a family's attention, especially when kids get so involved that they're on a traveling team with a schedule that resembles that of a college or professional team. Before you know it, Sunday mornings are spent on a field, not in a sanctuary, and dinner . . . well, that just never happens anymore. That's a great way to teach your children that being a star is more important than being a worshipper. Remember, Christlikeness comes first. Everything else is much further down on the list.

Most of the parents I talk to will tell me they believe that. "Of *course* sports are not as important as Christlikeness. I would never think such a thing." But remember that with children, it isn't what you think that's relevant; it's what you model. You can tell them daily or even hourly that God must come first in their lives, but if you're letting everything else come first, your words have very little impact. They embrace what you're really demonstrating.

That's a long way to say how important dinner together is, but it really is a relevant example in the lives of many American families. And it also affects the next way to develop and maintain communication.

(2) Bond at bedtime. This is especially important when your children are young, but even now that mine are grown, I still kiss them good night whenever we're staying in the same home or saying good-bye. When they're small, read them a story. And if you *really* want to endear yourself to them, make up a story, even basing a character on your child in a story just for him. What you put into his mind at bedtime are like deposits in his relational and spiritual bank accounts with you and God.

I used to make up stories for my children that were so wild we never knew how they were going to turn out. I'd get halfway through, realize how late it was, and tell them they'd have to wait until the next night for the conclusion. I had no idea how that conclusion would go, and it didn't matter. They loved the bedtime adventure. Sometimes it would involve tickling and pillow-fighting (especially on weekends, when bedtime hyperactivity wouldn't have far-reaching consequences into the next morning). But it would almost always involve at least a story and some tender words and kisses. There's no better way to bond with a young child than helping her feel secure in your love as she drifts off to sleep. And if your children are older, try to find some age-appropriate way to connect with them before bedtime, whether it's a talk about their day or a prayer about their tomorrow. One way or another, let them go to sleep with a pleasant reminder of your love for them.

(3) Plan shared experiences. Build memories, go camping, go to Disney World, play basketball in the driveway, go out for a late-night milk shake . . . use your imagination. There are numerous ways to share meaningful experiences with your children. There will come a time when meaningful experiences with their peers will become a higher priority for them than meaningful experiences with you—that's a natural stage of the maturing process—but the ones you make happen when you have the opportunity will last a lifetime.

One of my kids once went on an overnight project with his class, and parents were invited to chaperone. I volunteered out of sheer commitment to my son. The kids were put on an old-fashioned sailboat with a real captain. They dressed in uniforms and spent the night as the crew. I was up all night with preteens ordering me around like crazy, and I was freezing. But I can still remember it to this day, and so can my child. Planned experiences like that go a long way toward creating a long-lasting bond.

6. *Meaningful touch.* Touch is a powerful way to deepen your bond with your child. Some of the most effective vehicles of love in the world are human hands and arms. Touching, loving, and holding your children have an incredible effect on them. Hug them spontaneously or give them a high five when you're proud of them. Give them a quick kiss on the cheek (when it won't humiliate them in front of their friends). And for dads, wrestle with them on the floor when they're small—the more, the better. Have you ever wondered

why kids like to wrestle? It isn't because they have ambitions of getting in a ring one day as a professional wrestler. They want to touch you, and they want you to touch them. Tussling is a great way for them to get that touch, and it's a lot easier for them to provoke a wrestling match than ask for a hug. The playfulness of that kind of touch promotes a lasting emotional bond.

I can remember times when my daughter was little that I'd give my wife a hug while she was trying to cook dinner. We husbands often want to sneak in a hug and a kiss at inconvenient times, don't we? And wives try to brush us off because, frankly, we're getting in the way. But I would tell Theresa that I was doing it for the kids, modeling a healthy marriage for them. So she'd put her things down and turn around and hug me. My little girl would run up to us and say, "I want to do a sandwich!" Then she'd squeeze in between us.

What was she really saying? "I want to feel life and love around me; I want to feel safe with the people who love me." Children feed off the evidence of love you show in your home, especially through touch.

Don't ever stop hugging. The tendency of men in our culture is to stop hugging their daughters when they start to develop as young women. That's a weird thing for a man; you wake up one day and your little girl isn't a little girl anymore. She has become an attractive woman. It's very important to respect her woman-hood and only hug her appropriately, but it's also very important to keep hugging her. If your little girl doesn't get positive, appropriate male attention, she'll find male attention elsewhere, and it won't always be positive or appropriate. You are her primary male relationship, and she needs the kind of loving, nonsexual touch that will create a deep bond between you.

I was talking on the phone with my daughter not long after she went away to college, and I asked her what she missed most since being away from home. I was just making conversation, but her response brought me to tears: "Papa, I miss your hugs. I miss feeling safe and loved and special, like when you hug me. The first thing I want to do when you come to visit is get a big hug." Dads, hug your daughters!

7. *Have fun together.* In our home during the kids' formative years, we rarely watched any TV Monday through Friday. We just turned it off. By eight o'clock, my kids had run out of other things to do, so they would come up with their own entertainment. They all have musical talent, and they were motivated to develop it mainly because they weren't glued to the TV. I'm convinced that boredom is a blessing from God; it's a precursor to creativity. After listening to my kids complain for fifteen minutes about having nothing to do, I would find them reading a book, lifting weights, picking a guitar, or writing in their journals. We also played board games together and just goofed around and had fun. Sometimes we'd play basketball in the driveway and lose track of time. We'd look up in the sky, see all the stars, and spontaneously thank God for loving us and giving us a good time together. That's a thirty-second prayer that's connected with life as we lived it, and it probably had much more impact than a rigid devotional. That time together also had much more entertainment value than anything on TV.

You know what kids learn from a family experience like stargazing? That all of life is holy, and every moment can be an act of worship. *Especially* the fun moments.

8. *Pray together.* Pray at the table, pray at bedtime, pray during a crisis, pray when you're just having fun and are grateful about it. When you hear a siren go by, let your kids know someone somewhere may be hurting, and pray for them.

As she was growing up, my daughter and I formed a habit.

Whenever we got in the car together we'd pray for safety and for whatever we were going to do when we got to our destination. It was an unplanned thing, and usually it just happened. One time a few years ago, I turned the keys without even thinking about the prayer, and she said, "Aren't we going to pray?" It was so natural to her that she noticed when it was missing.

When the children were younger and our family was all together, we used to designate one night a week to have a slightly more formal dinner. We would brief each other on what was going on in our lives and then go around the table asking for prayer requests. After taking some time to pray for each other, we'd clean up the dishes and go get ice cream. It was scheduled, but it wasn't otherworldly. It was serious, but it was followed by a celebration. It integrated spirituality with life. We came before God, encouraged one another to live godly lives, modeled the joy and power of Christ to each other, and had a lot of fun doing it.

Integrate spirituality with life.

When parents are able to express unconditional love, schedule time for their children, focus attention on them, look into their eyes, maintain ongoing communication, touch them meaning-

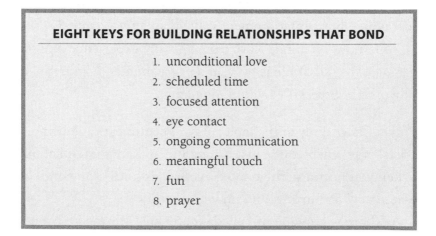

EIGHT KEYS FOR BUILDING RELATIONSHIPS THAT BOND

1. unconditional love
2. scheduled time
3. focused attention
4. eye contact
5. ongoing communication
6. meaningful touch
7. fun
8. prayer

fully, have fun together, and pray together, it's like putting money in a relational bank. And that investment gains a lot of interest over time.

Principle 4: Implement a Repair and Maintenance Plan

Life is a series of constant adjustments. Take your occupation, for example. What occupied your time ten years ago probably isn't the same thing that occupies your time today. Responsibilities shift, salaries fluctuate, and the dynamics of professional relationships change. The work you do requires a considerable amount of adaptation over the course of a lifetime.

Marriage is like that too. Relationships have seasons, and the couples who adjust to them get along a lot better than the couples who don't. Some seasons are light and fun, others are heavy and serious. Some seasons thrive on frivolity, and others depend on maturity. A couple who have been together for a long time can distinguish phases of the relationship in which each person's approach to the other evolved.

Parenting is no different. What worked with your children when they were two will not work with them when they are six, much less sixteen. What worked for one child may not work for another. Like a good coach at halftime, we have to know how to change our game plan based on the successes and failures we've already had. We need to be experts at developing ever-changing strategies.

> *Parenting Myth: If only we could find the right formula or how-to book, parenting would be straightforward.*
>
> **Parenting Reality:** No matter how well we're doing as parents, we constantly need to adapt our approach.

Effective parenting requires constant repair and ongoing maintenance. You can come up with the perfect plan—all the chores listed out, stars by the kids' names, homework checked off, plans for

39

which parent will help with math and which will help with English, memory verses for the entire next year plotted out on a chart—and even if the plan works for a while, there will be times when it doesn't. There will be times when you're sitting in the recliner and the kids start screaming at each other, and you just don't have the energy to discipline them. Things will go wrong.

In parenting, you never get in the groove and stay there. Your kids are never going to have it all together. In fact, I can remember only one or two times—ever—when all my children were doing well at the same time. Parenting is not neat, it's not clean, plans don't always work out, and constant revisions have to be made. I know books like this can tend to present parenting as a tidy, organized, and completely unrealistic endeavor. But in truth, it's messy.

Furthermore, every parent makes mistakes. That's why 1 John 1:9 is in the Bible: "If we confess our sins, he is faithful and just and will forgive us our sins and purify us from all unrighteousness." God understands everyone who is reading this book. He knows how we struggle and how we long to do better. He knows the private things in our hearts and the secret things of our pasts. He knows that most of us have yelled at the kids, been neglectful, and have tried so hard that we've gotten frustrated and been ready to give up.

God's message is this: "Hang in there. I'm at work. Labor together with Me, keep a clear focus on the target, and be very patient. Remember that you're the teacher. And even if you're not doing well, model how to come to Me and ask for forgiveness. Create a loving environment, and when you blow it, remember 1 John 1:9—I'll always forgive any sin you confess and purify you from it. I'll be faithful and just and give you what you need." It's amazing how God responds to our honesty before Him.

Parents who don't understand this principle will despair. Don't put this book down in discouragement, thinking you're not close to modeling a Christlike lifestyle for your children. You will have both good and bad seasons. We can beat ourselves up for all our short-comings and convince ourselves we're terrible parents and there's no hope. But God says the recognition of our failure is the first step to success. He compassionately calls us to come before Him and ask Him to forgive us of whatever needs His mercy and to help us get back on the right track. Just as we are to have a lot of grace in the way we teach our kids, He has a lot of grace in the way He teaches us. He wouldn't ask us to love our children unconditionally and neglect to do the same for us. So don't despair. There's hope, there's power, there's a Spirit who will help us, and there's a community of believers to support us. Own your sins, confess them, and He will cleanse and forgive.

> *God wouldn't ask us to love our children uncon-ditionally and neglect to do the same for us.*

FIVE POWERFUL WORDS

Because we live in this environment of grace, five words we each need to use regularly will powerfully transform our relationships with God and with our families: *"I'm sorry; please forgive me."*

It's never too late. Wherever you are as a parent—even if your kids are grown and you realize how much you could have done differently—there's hope. You may think you've really blown it, but God can take any mess in your life and turn it around. I could give you story after story of people who have blown it and still seen God redeem their mistakes. I'll give you just one, though—mine.

I had never opened a Bible until I was eighteen, and I married a woman who hadn't opened a Bible until she was twenty-five. Both of us came from dysfunctional families with alcoholics in them. We were a blended family because my wife came to the Lord only after she and her two boys were abandoned by her first husband. So we had no biblical background, no healthy past, and no history of observing mature Christian role models. In other words, we had no idea what we were doing.

Today Theresa and I have four kids who walk with God and love Him with all their hearts, even though we made plenty of mistakes along the way. I think there's a reason God wanted me to write a book like this: If He could help parents with a background like my wife's and mine raise kids who love God, there's hope for everyone.

So if all of this is new to you and you're struggling, keep reading. Now that we've laid the groundwork, we're going to learn from God's Word how to be an effective parent in a defective world.

Putting It into Practice

Look at the following eight keys to building a stronger bond with your children. Think of one way that you can incorporate each of these keys into your relationship this week.

EIGHT KEYS FOR BUILDING RELATIONSHIPS THAT BOND

1. Unconditional love _____

_____

_____

2. Scheduled time _____

_____

_____

3. Focused attention _____

_____

_____

4. Eye contact _____

_____

_____

5. Ongoing communication _____

_____

_____

6. Meaningful touch _____

_____

_____

7. Fun _____

_____

_____

8. Prayer _____

_____

_____

Take some time to reflect on your parenting. Can you identify one key attitude or behavior that, with God's help, you'd like to adjust? How might you begin to do so?

_____

_____

_____

_____

3 / How to Develop Your Child's Full Potential

I had been out of town for a few days. At the time, my youngest was four, the next youngest was ten, and my twins were sixteen. I came in late from my trip, and everyone was asleep. The way our house was laid out, I found that I could turn on the bathroom light, leave the door open, and see into their bedrooms. I had really missed them, so I tiptoed around and peeked into their rooms.

I opened the first door and looked at my four-year-old daughter. I don't know what it is about little girls, but they look like angels when they sleep. She was breathing rhythmically and looked so beautiful. I thought to myself, *What a privilege to be that little girl's dad.*

Then I went to the next bedroom and noticed that a ten-year-old boy doesn't look like an angel at all. I think he'd had a huge wrestling match with his pillow because the covers were all over the place, and he was scrunched up as if he'd had to fight for his position. I looked at him and thought, *Lord, what kind of dreams do You have for him? He has a ton of energy and passion. What do Your dreams for him look like?*

Then I looked into the twins' bedroom and thought, *How could they be born at the same time and be so different? What a joy to be the dad of such good young men now, no longer little boys.* And I came back out into the hall and felt what you've probably felt in similar moments: I had an overwhelming sense of privilege to be a parent and to bring human lives into the world.

That blissful thought was followed by a sudden rush of fear. What in the world was I going to do with these kids? They needed to become all God wanted them to be, and I feared that I didn't have what it took. Was I being too hard on them? too soft? too firm? too gentle? Those are questions we all ask from time to time, and they usually come up when we're scared to death of our parenting responsibilities.

God's Dream

Let's expand on a truth we touched on in the first chapter: God has a dream for your child, just as He has one for you. And His dream is more wonderful and more exciting than you could possibly envision.

How do I know that? Jeremiah 29:11 promises a good plan for His people, and Ephesians 3:20 says that God "is able to do immeasurably more than all we ask or imagine." Put the two together, and it's clear that God's purposes apply not only to the church, but also to every little boy and girl out there—including the ones in your home. That really hit home for me that night I got in late from a trip and peeked into their bedrooms. There was a plan for each one of those precious children, and my wife and I were God's stewards of the plan.

How, then, can you as a steward help your children reach their full potential? How can you cooperate with God in such a way that

His Spirit uses your life and His Word so that His purposes for your children become reality? There are four keys that we'll look at in this chapter and the next.

Key One: Understand Their Primary Needs

The most important thing you can do to help your children reach their potential is to meet their two primary emotional needs: *significance* and *security*. In other words, your kids need to know that they matter, and they need to know that they're safe.

You may not be aware of it, but your children—whether they're two years old or twenty—are constantly asking if you love them. It's not that they walk up to you and verbalize that question. But much of their behavior, both positive and negative, is designed to elicit a response out of you that communicates, *I love you and you matter. You're valuable and significant.*

> *Your kids need to know that they matter, and they need to know that they're safe.*

Your children are also always asking another nonverbal question: *Where are my boundaries?* They find security in the limits you place on them, and they are constantly testing those limits to see where they are. Wherever you draw the boundaries, they will spend some time every day pushing to see how solid those boundaries are. If you were to draw a line in the sand and tell them not to cross it, do you know what they'd do? They would get as close to it as they could— some would step over, some would put a toe across, and some would just nudge the edge of it. But every one of them would test it. They need to know just how secure your security measures are.

When you repeatedly answer the question "Do you love me?" by your words and actions, you're telling your children that they're significant. And when you draw clear boundaries by your words and actions and let them know you're in charge, you're cultivating their security.

Learn to see those two issues as guardrails. Determine to pour love into your kids in abundance even as you make it clear that as long as they're under your roof, they will have to live in a way that honors God, parents, and siblings.

We see God as the very first parent doing the same thing. In Genesis 1, following every stage of Creation, He kept saying how good and beautiful it was. Then He created male and female in His own image, the crown of Creation, and said that they were *very* good. He pointed out all the things He had made for them, all the land and fruitfulness He had given them, and treated it all as an expression of His love. He walked with them in the cool of the evening, He talked with them, He built intimacy with them, and He bestowed on them incredible significance and value.

But God also let Adam and Eve know He was in charge. He set up a boundary, making it clear that eating from a certain tree was forbidden. He literally gave them the world and then told them how far they could go with that gift. His love, for them and for us, produces significance, and His boundaries produce security.

He's still doing that, isn't He? Over and over again in Scripture, He says, "I love you, I love you, I love you." But He also never compromises His standards. He has a clear vision of what's best for us, and He insists on our conforming to that vision—not because He likes to dampen our spirits, but because He delights in setting us up for His best. If we'll listen, we'll hear God constantly answering our two questions: "Yes, I love you. Yes, you're safe in My hands."

Your children are going to have a hard time hearing that message from an invisible Father if they don't hear it from you first. Answer their questions early and often. Remember in the back of your mind that every moment of every day, whether your children are two, ten, or eighteen, in one way or another they are asking you if you really love them, and they are asking you how far they can go.

Key Two: Recognize Their Primary Responsibility

The second key to developing your children's full potential is to recognize that their foremost responsibility is to learn obedience. While they are living under your roof, they have a primary duty: to learn to obey.

That's spelled out in Ephesians 6:1: "Children, obey your parents in the Lord, for this is right." Paul points out that the commandment to honor parents is the first commandment with a promise. The Bible is filled with all kinds of commandments for leaders, husbands, wives, servants, and all kinds of people. Everybody from every walk of life gets instructions. But I can find only one command directed at children: obey.

This word *obey* in the New Testament is a compound word derived from *hypo* (to be under) and *akouo* (to hear): in other words, "to be under the hearing of." Obedience is not about parents being strong and domineering, making the kids do exactly what they say out of fear. Obedience is teaching your children to be under the hearing of your voice so that when you speak, they obey. And while it's true that they need to obey simply because you are the authority in their lives, the goal is for them to obey out of love, dependency, and trust. Genuine obedience is submitting to the word of another, whether it's God or parents. But healthy obedience is submitting not exclusively out of fear, but out of love and trust. There are times, especially when children are young, that they must obey simply because you said so. The ultimate goal, however, is to create a deeper motivation.

While your children are living under your roof, they have a primary duty: to learn to obey.

If you were asked in a survey what your number one goal is for your children, what would you say? The average parent wouldn't even think to say, "For them to obey." Yet this is the *only* command for children God gives in His Word. They have one critical assign-

ment: "Children, obey your parents." It's absolutely crucial
to understand that this is a child's primary goal in life.

> *Parenting Myth: My children's primary responsibility is to
> juggle the schoolwork and extracurricular activities that will
> make them well-rounded, successful adults.*

> **Parenting Reality**: My children's primary responsibility
> is to learn healthy obedience.

As a young parent, I came very close to learning this lesson the
hard way. My ignorance of—or indifference to—God's command
to teach children to obey almost cost the life of one of my sons.
Our family was taking a walk around a safe residential area one day
when our older boys were about four or five. My son Eric had his
favorite tennis shoes on, and he would point down to them, give
us a wave, and run ahead of us. Whenever he got to a driveway,
I'd yell out, "Eric, stop," and he'd look, wave, and keep right on
going. I didn't really expect him to stop, and he knew it. At one
point, we were walking along a hedged yard. I could see over the
hedge, but Eric couldn't. We were holding the hand of our other
son, just enjoying our walk, and I saw a car coming out of the
driveway as Eric neared the end of the hedge. He and the car were
on a perfect collision course.

As you can imagine, my heart almost jumped out of my chest.
I yelled, "Eric, stop!" and of course he didn't. Why would he? I had
never taught him that obedience to my voice was critical. The car
zoomed by and narrowly missed him. I ran over and grabbed my
precious son. "Eric, you need to understand that when I tell you
to do something, you have to do it! You just scared me to death."
I realized at that moment that I hadn't been nearly serious enough
about teaching and disciplining my kids to obey.

Children are excellent students of their parents, if you haven't noticed. Have you ever watched them at the grocery store? Every second, it's, "Mom, Mom, can we get this?" And Mom constantly has to say, "No, not today." When she gets tired of saying that, though, she caves. "All right, put it in the cart." Or the classic example, in my opinion, is when a couple visit their friend's house and tell the kids, who have spent three hours trashing every room in the house, that it's time to clean up and get ready to go.

"Bobby, it's time to help pick up all the toys. We're going to leave in just a minute." But Bobby and his friend don't move. Not even a budge.

Five minutes later, the command is repeated, but this time louder and with a little anger in the tone. Still, not even a hint that it was heard.

Then the parents move from the kitchen table to the hallway, still talking, but putting on coats and obviously about to walk out the door. Now they scream at their son in obvious frustration.

"Bobby, I told you, pick up those toys right now! We have to leave." And Bobby turns to his friend and says, "I think we may be about to leave. I'll see you later."

Children know when their parents' command means, "You have to do this now," and when it means, "You'll really have to do this after I've said it the third or fourth time." In effect, a child who knows when "do this" doesn't really mean "do this" has trained his parents, not been trained by them.

It isn't very hard to walk over, get down to eye level with a five-year-old, and say calmly, firmly, and under control, "Bobby, we're about to leave. Do you understand that? I want you to pick up the toys right now." And if he doesn't obey, consequences should immediately follow. That child will learn that when a parent gives a clear instruction in a calm voice, it matters. And the reason this is so important, beside the fact that his safety depends on it, is that if a child can't learn to obey a parent who is visible, he'll never learn to obey a God who isn't. Whatever attitude your children have toward your voice, that's probably how they'll respond to God's when they're older.

Do you understand that obedience is God's channel of blessing? It's the highway that God asks us as children to stay on so we can experience the highest and best for our lives. If we don't teach our children to obey, we're setting them up to miss out on God's blessings. We're denying them the training they will one day need to hear God's still, small voice and act on it. When God whispers to them, "This relationship is bad for you," or "Don't get in the car with those guys," they'll keep right on running just as Eric ran toward the driveway, completely unaware of the danger. They won't really believe that voice is serious.

> *If a child can't learn to obey a parent who is visible, he'll never learn to obey a God who isn't.*

If you think I'm exaggerating the importance of this, look at what Jesus says about the relationship between love and obedience: "Whoever has my commands and obeys them, he is the one who loves me. He who loves me will be loved by my Father, and I too will love him and show myself to him" (John 14:21). The stakes can't get any higher than that. For the sake of their relationship with God Himself, teach your children to obey the first time. It will take effort, practice, and patience, but it is well worth it. Let's look at how this process of obedience works with children at various stages of development.

Key Three: Obedience Is a Process

Obedience is a developmental process. You don't just tell children one time how important it is to obey, enforce their obedience, and then expect them to obey from that day forward. They will test their limits periodically, and they will need reminders that you're serious about your word. You also can't start emphasizing obedience when they're twelve and expect them to get the hang of it right away. If they're not in the habit of submitting to you, it may be a little traumatic for them to start. They'll get it eventually, but it's a process.

That process takes perseverance, and it takes the understanding that kids develop in different ways at different times. Even Jesus had to learn to obey. Hebrews 5:8 says that "although he was a son, he learned obedience from what he suffered." He was perfect humanity, and yet He had to learn. How? Through suffering. We're told that He "grew in wisdom and stature, and in favor with God and men" (Luke 2:52). His obedience included intellectual growth (wisdom), physical growth (stature), spiritual growth (favor with God), and social growth (favor with men). Even for the Son of God, it was a process.

Remember that your method for teaching obedience will differ with the personality and age of your child. Toddlers don't learn obedience the same way teenagers do. Lawrence Kohlberg, a psychologist who spent his life studying the development of children, discovered distinct stages of development in which the learning process differed from age to age.[2]

When children are small, for example, they are very concrete thinkers. They believe they are the center of the universe. When they play peekaboo, they think that you can't see them when their eyes are covered because they can't see you. When a Sunday school teacher asks them if they want Jesus to live in their hearts, they'll say, "I don't think He'll fit." There's no sense of the abstract. When they are young, they learn in black-and-white, in terms of what they can see and touch and taste. But by the time they're sixteen or seventeen, they can be very abstract in their thinking. They can learn concepts, draw inferences from contexts, and express potentiality.

We aren't normally conscious of these levels of learning when we teach our kids. Our biggest problem in teaching obedience to young children is that we talk too much. And then when they're teenagers, we tend to talk too little.

When they're young, our goal should be simply to teach basic information and the rules of life—what's right and wrong. "God loves it when we obey," "Tell the truth," "Don't hit your sister," "Stealing is wrong," "Don't touch the stove," "Don't run into the street." We're forming a foundation by focusing on the "what."

As they get a little older, we focus on the "who." We want them to understand right and wrong, but we want them to understand it in the context of our love for them and their love for us. We want them to realize that life is about a relationship with God. Young kids can't grasp much of that, but between the ages of about six and ten, they begin to understand that obedience, whether to you or to God, is a relationship issue.

> *Our biggest problem in teaching obedience to young children is that we talk too much. And then when they're teenagers, we tend to talk too little.*

Then as kids get into their early teens, they want to do more and more. They push for more levels of freedom and responsibility, especially as peer pressure begins to become a more powerful force. At this point, when they ask why or why not, it's generally not a good idea to say, "Because I said so." That works with five-year-olds, not with teenagers. You have the same authority at both ages, but you should exercise it differently. A fifteen-year-old knows what the rules are but now also needs to know the rationale behind them. God has been stimulating their brains to understand how life works. You have to give them the reasons behind your rules.

When they say, "So-and-so's parents let him do that," you had

SPIRITUAL FORMATION AND MENTAL DEVELOPMENT

	Rules	Relationship	Reason	Resolve
AGE:	0–4 or 5	6–7	11–12	16–17
	concrete thinking ⟶ adult abstract thinking			

better give them a better answer than, "I'm not so-and-so's parent. I'm yours." You have a golden opportunity to say, "Look, I know your friends are going to that movie, but it has way too much sex and violence in it. The issue is not who else is going or whether you can get by with it. You need to think about whether it's pleasing to God. What would this do to your relationship with Him? How would you feel about it afterward? Do you think you'd have a clean conscience? Which choice do you think God is most likely to bless?" Help them ask the hard questions. By doing this, you teach them that obedience is God's channel of blessing and that the reason you're telling them no is because you love them. That kind of interaction trains them to make the responsible decisions that adults need to make.

When they're in their late teens, you take your focus off the what, the who, and the why, and you let them begin making decisions. You remind them of the value of their beliefs, you walk them through the implications of their choices, and you get them to the point where they can live responsibly before they leave your house so you can sleep a lot easier afterward. They will make some bad decisions—that's guaranteed—but they'll make them in a place where you can coach them, forgive them, and help them respond positively to the consequences. The goal is that they develop personal convictions that are based on their own relationship with Christ and that will sustain and guide them whether you're around or not.

A RECIPE FOR CONVICTIONS

How do children develop convictions that are biblical and that they can embrace as their own? I believe there is a very clear process by which this occurs in all of our lives. First we need to learn information, to receive knowledge. Then we are to understand the context of love behind that instruction. Finally, we need wisdom, the biblical and logical reasons behind all that we've learned, and the skill to apply that wisdom in real-life situations. When you add those elements together, it results in a set of convictions, or deep-seated beliefs and values, that govern behavior and decision making.

KNOWLEDGE + LOVE + WISDOM = CONVICTIONS

During the developmental process, you impart to your children knowledge, love, and wisdom—the what, the who, and the why—so that when they leave your home, they are prepared to make great decisions because they've transferred their trust and dependency from you to their relationship with Jesus. They have a solid foundation of rules, relationship, and resolve that will powerfully direct their lives toward greater maturity in God's Kingdom.

One issue with my kids, for example, that illustrates this dynamic particularly well is how they learned to guard what they put in their minds. The first step was to make them aware of what was good to watch or listen to and what was not. Over time, it became more than an issue of following a rule; they learned that exposing themselves to harmful media would cause pain for their mother and me because we cared for them. When they were later able to observe the lifestyle of friends who had spent years feeding their minds with junk, they understood the wisdom behind our standards. The progression of that issue—from a matter of information to a matter of relationship to a matter of observable experience—led to their own internal convictions.

TWO VITAL PRINCIPLES

You don't have to be a degree-holding psychologist to navigate your children's developmental stages. If I were to boil down a parent's response to Kohlberg's findings on the stages of learning, two principles would sum it up: the principles of readiness and responsibility.

The principle of readiness means to teach children what they are mentally and emotionally capable of learning. If I saw a parent down on one knee explaining the process of sanctification to a three-year-old, I would be almost as frustrated as the child would be. I'd know the kid just wanted to ride his tricycle but Mom or Dad wouldn't let him. Deep explanations and ten-minute lectures aren't really needed at that age.

At the other end of the spectrum, I've seen parents tell a seventeen-year-old, who presumably should be learning to make his own decisions, "That's what I said, and that's the way it's going to be." That's just as frustrating to a kid. He'll end up going to his room, slamming the door, and the parents end up with a major problem.

Those may be exaggerated examples, but we often do those kinds of things in more subtle ways. We need to teach our children what they're able to understand—not more, not less.

Imagine your child as a kite. When he's small, you release just a little of the string and provide lots of oversight and protection because he'll crash if given too much leeway. You have to create a lot of movement to keep the kite up in the air, and it can be hard work. But you wouldn't let go of hundreds of feet of string and expect him to try to manage himself in the high winds.

As your child grows, you let out a little more of the string, and then a little more. The kite may begin to take a dip, so you step in and make sure he doesn't crash. When he's back up, you let out a little more string. Eventually, your child is able to fly on his own, and he needs less supervision from you. There are seasons in flying a kite, and you have to be aware of them.

You also have to be sensitive to the individuality of your children. They will ride the wind differently from their peers, and probably even differently from their own brothers and sisters. There's no cookie-cutter way to soar. There are box kites, winged kites, kites with long tails, kites with short tails, and kites with all sorts of designs and decorations. The strength of the wind varies from day to day and from hour to hour. A parent who comes up with a formula is going to have the right formula only part of the time. The rest of the time, the formula will be inappropriate. Parenting requires adaptation to the child's learning style, the environment around him, and the capacity of the child to learn at that given moment. Following the principle of readiness requires understanding how your child thinks.

If I said, for example, that your child needs to be able to babysit for her toddler brother by the time she's thirteen, some of you would think I was crazy, and others would think I'm stating the obvious. Some children are able to handle that responsibility at an early age, and some need to wait a little longer. There are many variables involved: her temperament, how much hands-on experience she's had, her willingness, the toddler's tendencies, and a host of other things. There's no rule for such a responsibility. It depends on the kite you're flying.

You can apply that principle to a multitude of other issues. When should a young child be expected to dress herself? When should a teenager be given his own checking account? Your answers for your children will differ from the answers other parents give to their children. Why? Because your children have unique personalities and mature at different rates. You have to know your kite well.

The principle of responsibility does have a common denominator, however, regardless of your child's tendencies. Never do for your chil-

dren what they can do for themselves. You want them to grow up and be responsible, and the only way for them to do that is to practice responsibility. If your goal is to raise children who can take care of themselves and their own children one day, then parenting must be a process of transferring trust, accountability, and dependability to them little by little until they are fully mature. That needs to start early and be pursued often.

This is especially hard for mothers. The nurturing instinct is so strong that they sometimes don't let go when they should. At some point, the desire to nurture must give way to the desire to see independently healthy children. There's an appropriate time for mother eagles to nudge their eaglets out of the nest.

> *Never do for your children what they can do for themselves.*

The PTA's 1985 National Outstanding Educator of the Year, Gene Bedley, has written many articles and books on this subject. How does he say to teach responsibility?

When I turn it on . . . I turn it off.
When I unlock something . . . I lock it up.
When I drop something . . . I pick it up.
When I break something . . . I repair it.
When I open something . . . I close it.
When I make a mess . . . I clean it up.
When I make a promise . . . I keep my promise.
When I find something . . . I return it.
When I borrow something . . . I give it back.
When I take it out . . . I put it back.
When I'm assigned to a task . . . I complete it on time.
When I earn money . . . I spend and invest it wisely.[3]

Your job as a parent is not to make your children's life work out all the time. It's to put the ball in their court—to transfer responsibility. The following questions may make some of us squirm a little bit, but they provide a practical test to evaluate whether you're increasing responsibility as a child grows:

1. Do all your children have chores that are clearly laid out?
2. If you have a child under ten, who makes his bed? Does he brush his own teeth? Who cleans up his room? Does he ever help set the table? help separate laundry into whites and darks?
3. If you have a child in junior high, who wakes her up each day? Who gets her ready for school? Does she ever vacuum the house? wash the dishes? clean the bathroom?
4. If you have a fifteen- or sixteen-year-old, who does his laundry? Does he share responsibility for cooking the meals sometimes? for yard work and household maintenance?
5. If your teenagers have a baby sibling, do they ever feed her? change her diaper?

You won't know your child's capabilities for household tasks until you've shifted the responsibility for them. You need to be sensitive to when you're pushing too hard, but don't be afraid to push your kids firmly. Let the kite string out as far as you can so they can learn to fly as quickly as they need to.

One of the greatest mysteries of American parenthood is why parents who are working sixty hours a week and juggling their kids' soccer practice schedules and music lessons are frantically at work in the kitchen while a fully able teenager sits in front of a video game saying, "Hey, Mom, is dinner ready yet?" We've raised a whole generation of twentysomethings hanging out in the back bedroom wondering what they'll be served for breakfast, lunch, and dinner. There's something wrong with that picture.

Kids need to have age-appropriate responsibilities, and they need to suffer the consequences of not meeting those responsibilities. Remember, any time you regularly do something for your children that they can do for themselves, you make them an emotional cripple. All of my kids got their own alarm clock when they hit junior high. It was their responsibility, not mine or Theresa's, to get themselves up, get dressed, and get ready for school. Yes, they missed the bus once or twice, but it only took a couple of times before they learned not to push the snooze button too often. When motivated, children are remarkably quick to take responsibility upon themselves, and insisting that they do sure beats the kind of nagging and cajoling that ruins relationships. There's no reason to carry the weight of micromanaging their lives.

The way to transfer responsibility to your children is to let them watch what you're doing and then give them an opportunity to do it themselves. Then once they know how, insist that they incorporate their knowledge into their daily routines. My kids used to watch my wife cook dinner, then they helped her, and before long they tested their skills by cooking for us. My sons, as new fathers, knew how to take care of their children right away because they had helped with their baby sister years before. Changing diapers was not a problem for them—they'd had practice.

This is also one of the most effective ways to build self-esteem in a child. Many parents think added responsibility creates pressure and lowers esteem, but it actually has the opposite effect. As much as they act like they want to be waited on, kids crave the ability to do things on their own. When we keep doing things for them that they can do for themselves, we're communicating our lack of trust in their competence. Few things are more crippling than that. That does nothing to prepare them to survive in a world where responsibility is expected. If we don't want to have thirty-year-old dependents on our hands, we must strategically and intentionally cultivate their independence from us. We'll be a lot happier, and our children will be a lot happier.

Another reason to be zealous about transferring responsibility to our children is how it affects their relationship with God. People really only seek dependence on God when they feel their _____ sense of need. A child whose parents always take care of everything for him has very little emotional need for God. Why would he depend on an invisible Lord when he can depend on his visible parents? If Mom and Dad are always cleaning up after their child so that he never has to suffer the consequences of his actions, he'll never understand the cause and effect of sin or of the choices he makes in life. And if he never understands that, he will never seek God as his forgiver, helper, and strength.

People really only seek dependence on God when they feel their sense of need. A child whose parents always take care of everything for him has very little emotional need for God.

A WORD ABOUT DISCIPLINE

We'll get deeper into the nuts and bolts of discipline in chapter 5, but we have to touch on it here in the context of teaching responsibility to children. Ephesians 6:4 (NASB) says, "Do not provoke your children to anger, but bring them up in the discipline and instruction of the Lord." The word for *discipline* is also translated in other places in the New Testament as "to train" or "to chastise." It's a very strong word, and it always implies what is *done* to the child. The word for *instruction* is translated in other places as "warn," "counsel," "admonish," "encourage," "urge," and "implore." It always implies what is *said* to the child.

Interestingly, the word order used in this passage—"discipline" and then "instruction"—fits our latest and best research on child development. When kids are small, you don't talk a lot. You discipline with action (rewards and consequences), because they don't understand much else. As they grow and learn to communicate and conceptualize, teaching (verbal instruction) plays a more prominent role. You communicate not only what you expect, but the why behind it. You let consequences or actions keep them on track, but their comprehension of expectations is now rooted in a fuller understanding of the logic, reasons, and relational basis for those expectations.

Where Are You?

Think about where you are with your children for a moment. You know that their two primary needs are significance and security. And you know that while being a great athlete or musician can be desirable, your most important task as a parent is to help your kids learn obedience—not as a switch to turn on, but as a developmental process to persevere in. With that groundwork in mind, consider where you are right now. Look at the chart on page 64 and ask yourself how you're teaching your kids at this point in their lives.

Are you cooperating with the principle of readiness? with the principle of responsibility? Are there any midcourse adjustments you need to make?

If changes are needed, ask God to help you come up with some specific steps you can take to redirect your children back toward the bull's-eye. Remember that having the right information doesn't transform a life; application does. Whatever steps you need to make to get back on course, determine to trust God and take them.

He will help you every step of the way if you let Him. He didn't just leave us with instructions and hope we would be able to figure them out on our own. God has a lot at stake in your abilities as a parent, and He will teach and enable you as you walk your children through the process of learning obedience. That takes time, and you'll need to ask Him specifically for guidance. But He uses your times of seeking direction to draw you closer to Him. Remember, He's parenting you while you're parenting your children.

Putting It into Practice

Ask each of your children what kinds of things make him or her feel special and loved. It may take some time and conversing to get your child to open up. Perhaps you can ask your child to name one or two things you already do that make him or her feel loved—or that your child wishes you would start doing (or wishes you would do more). What key discovery did you make?

_____

_____

_____

_____

Next ask each of your children what kinds of things make him or her feel secure. Your child may not give the "right" answer ("When you enforce the boundaries"). But just listen and observe any sensitivities, fears, concerns, or other issues you haven't seen before. Did you discover anything new?

_____

_____

_____

_____

SPIRITUAL FORMATION AND MENTAL DEVELOPMENT

	Rules	Relationship	Reason	Resolve
AGE:	0–4 or 5	6–7	11–12	16–17
concrete thinking ⟶ adult abstract thinking				

Look at the Spiritual Formation and Mental Development chart on page 64 and identify the level of instruction (rules, relationship, reason, or resolve) that correlates with each of your children's current ages.

Child's name: _____ Type of instruction: _____

Child's name: _____ Type of instruction: _____

Child's name: _____ Type of instruction: _____

Child's name: _____ Type of instruction: _____

Child's name: _____ Type of instruction: _____

What specific responsibilities does each of your children have in your home? for their own room? housework? pets? meals? laundry?

_____

_____

_____

_____

_____

_____

_____

_____

_____

_____

_____

How can you be more effective in helping them take responsibilities for themselves and their actions?

_____

_____

_____

_____

4 / God's Process for Teaching Obedience

Theresa and I got married when her twins were four years old. We got home from the honeymoon, and immediately I had fatherly responsibilities. Not only did I need to adjust to married life, I needed to adjust to family life. I wanted to be a great dad, and I worked hard to become one. But what do you do when you have to learn how to discipline two boys without having any prior experience raising kids? Some parenting instincts, like provision and protection, are natural. But instincts only get you moving in the right direction. They have to be turned into skills, which must be learned and developed. You can't just flip a switch after the honeymoon.

For me, learning how to be a good parent involved constant prayer, learning from other Christian parents through observation and by asking specific questions, investigating what the Bible says about parenting, and a lot of trial and error. Over time, I learned how to improve my skills as a father. I found the next key very effective in sharpening skills.

Key Four: Provide the Necessary Resources

A child doesn't learn obedience by accident. It takes an intentional effort by the parent, and that effort requires a commitment. Every parent who wants to train a child in obedience must commit to providing the necessary resources for that child to learn to obey. That's a huge, long-term process.

What would you think of a parent who had a great income but neglected to provide food, clothing, and shelter for his kids? What would you think of a very rich couple who lived in a huge mansion but gave their children only a small closet-sized room, or went on expensive vacations but never took the kids along? You would instinctively see that as selfish and neglectful, wouldn't you? Then what would you think of parents who have every spiritual resource the Most High King has to offer—blessing upon blessing from the riches of heaven—yet don't share those spiritual resources and set their children up for a fruitful, eternal life?

Most parents are totally committed to providing the necessities of life—and even the luxuries, when possible—for their children. We want to give them everything they need to be successful in life. Yet we often neglect to give our children the very thing they need to put themselves in a position to be blessed and favored by God: humble obedience that flows out of faith and dependence on Him. And the sad part of our neglect is that we have the tools, the words and riches of Christ, to share with them. We lack nothing of what we really need.

It's ironic that the intensity and single-mindedness required for the kind of success that allows us to share material resources with our kids are often contrary to the qualities needed to be an effective

We often neglect to give our children the very thing they need to put themselves in a position to be blessed and favored by God: humble obedience that flows out of faith and dependence on Him.

parent. You can have a highly successful career and yet lack all the skills necessary to be a successful parent. A prominent business magazine reported that the percentage of teenagers who undergo treatment for psychiatric or substance abuse problems each year is more than twice as high among children of executives than among children of nonexecutives in the same companies.[4] There's more to parenting than providing food, clothing, and shelter—even if we provide gourmet food, designer clothing, and shelter in the toniest neighborhood. Money and success are nice to have, but those are not the resources that produce godly children. Only the right spiritual resources can do that.

Our culture doesn't push us in that direction. Just the opposite, in fact. Most parents are persuaded that if they provide for their children financially, give them nice clothes, put them in good schools, and arm them with the latest computers, they've done their job. But because a child's number one responsibility is to learn obedience, those other advantages are further down on the list of importance. None of those things will cultivate the right spirit in a child. A different set of resources is needed.

GOD GIVES YOU THE TOOLS

Five tools that will help children learn obedience can be found in Deuteronomy 6. That passage was originally addressed to the people of Israel after they had wandered in the wilderness for forty years and were about to enter the Promised Land. Not long before he died, Moses reviewed all the instructions God had given them and urged them to remain faithful to His commands forever. In chapter 6, Moses gives the foundational tools for obedience that we also need to understand:

Hear, O Israel! The LORD is our God, the LORD is one! You shall love the LORD your God with all your heart and with all your soul and with all your might. These words, which I am commanding

*you today, shall be on your heart. You shall teach them diligently
to your sons and shall talk of them when you sit in your house
and when you walk by the way and when you lie down and when
you rise up. You shall bind them as a sign on your hand and they
shall be as frontals on your forehead. You shall write them on
the doorposts of your house and on your gates. (Deuteronomy
6:4-9, NASB)*

1. *Doctrinal truth.* "The LORD is our God, the LORD is one." This is
not just an informational statement. In a world full of gods of all
shapes and sizes and *isms* from every human perspective imagin-
able, Moses throws down the theological gauntlet and says,
"There's only one God to whom we are responsible."

First and foremost, we are to teach our kids doctrinal truth.
That's resource number one. In a culture that preaches and practices relativism, we nail down certain truths that our children
can stake their lives on. We teach them the difference between
right and wrong; who God is; why He sent Jesus into the world;
and that Jesus is fully God and fully man, the Savior of the
world, the Way and Truth and Life. Doctrinal truth is a necessary foundation for kids who live in this sea of relativity, who
listen to popular music and watch TV, who have a hundred
friends who tell them a million different ways to do things.
Moms and dads need to teach what's true and right.

Doctrinal truth is a necessary foundation for kids who live in a sea of relativity.

If the idea of understanding doctrinal
truth intimidates you, be encouraged.
I came from a non-Christian background
and had never read the Bible until I was
eighteen. I was able to learn scriptural
truths by digging into the Bible and asking
God to teach me. You can do the same. (For a list of helpful
resources, see page 81.)

2. *Personal Devotion.* "You shall love the LORD your God." This is the ultimate purpose for everyone—parents and children alike. Only parents who love God with every bit of energy they have are in a position to teach the true meaning of obedience to their kids, and only children who come to understand that the foundation of obedience is love will learn to obey from the right motivation.

Our own personal devotion is a vital resource for our kids. Children must see in their parents what it means to love the Lord. This goes back to the principle of modeling what you want them to become. Your kids need to accidentally catch you praying over a passage with an open Bible in front of you. Late at night or early in the morning when they're supposed to be in bed but get up to go to the bathroom, they sometimes need to see you on your knees or talking with your spouse about God's will for your lives. When you get bad news, they need to see the tears you pour out to God. When you get good news, they need to see the celebration of a grateful heart. Over the course of their lives in your home, your children will see the habits of your life. If your acts of love toward God are habitual, your kids are much more likely to learn to love God too.

If you think you're too busy to practice these habits, think again. Your other loves get your attention, don't they? If you're like most people, you're not too busy to watch TV, follow the stats of your favorite team, read the newspaper, stay up-to-date with your favorite magazine, or read a gripping novel. If you can model those interests for your kids, surely you can model your devotion for the one true God.

If we practice our devotional life with reluctant obedience, our children will see that and develop the same attitude toward obedience. But if devotion to God is a priority and a passion, that's what will rub off on our kids. One of the most important tools we can give them is the example of our own wholehearted dedication to God.

3. *Biblical knowledge.* "These words . . . shall be on your heart." We are to live and breathe God's Word before we pass it on to our children. We have to know the Word of God; His commandments must be on our hearts.

There's a passage all my children know, and they didn't even have to memorize it because they heard it so often in our home. Whenever they were critical, mean-spirited, or sarcastic with each other, they would hear Ephesians 4:29: "Let no unwholesome word proceed out of your mouth, but only what is good for edification according to the need of the moment, that it may give grace to those that hear" (NASB). If that verse continued to be violated after a warning or two, they had to put one of their dimes into the missions jar. If the bickering still didn't stop, the stakes would go higher—a quarter or more. My children learned God's commands because His Word would be applied to their specific issues.

The average parent doesn't know where to go in the Bible to teach or correct his or her child. Unless he or she knows the Bible, however, teaching and correcting turns into a lot of trying harder, justifying more, and eventually yelling and screaming. The only way children can embrace biblical wisdom is to have it applied to their lives. A parent who doesn't know Scripture can't give a child that necessary tool. I encourage you to begin getting into the Bible regularly, selecting a version you can understand that includes some helpful notes and instruction. I used *The Daily Walk Bible* the first ten to fifteen years after I became a Christian; it set the biblical foundation for my parenting.

4. *Systematic instruction.* "You shall teach them diligently to your sons and shall talk of them." When should you teach your chil-

dren about obedience to God? When you sit in your house, when you walk, when you lie down, when you get up . . . in other words, all the time. It can't be accomplished in an hour of Sunday school each week.

"You shall teach them diligently" does not allow for a haphazard approach. This goes beyond a timely verse during a conversation in the car. While deliberate instruction is an important component of spiritual training, parents will differ in the methods they choose to teach their kids. In your home, you might meet one-on-one with each of your kids, taking them out for breakfast or ice cream once every week or two and doing a Bible study together. You might incorporate Bible stories into life's routines like bedtimes. You might also insist that every Tuesday night the family has devotions.

Speaking of devotions, this is one practice I strongly encourage you to incorporate into your family life. I believe family devotions should be brief, they should be focused, and they should be fun.[5] Being intentional about doing devotions requires following a consistent schedule. That's one of the most difficult things a parent has to do, and nearly every parent I know feels an enormous amount of guilt on this issue. Please don't beat yourself up over that. Forget the past. Just erase that guilt by confessing your shortcomings to the Lord, and then move on. Resolve to start family devotions now, even if you've failed in your past attempts. Start with a couple of nights a week, if aiming for seven and missing half of them makes you feel like a failure. Take some small steps toward the goal, and see what God will do with your efforts.

I have just one caution about systematic instruction: Don't make the mistake of trying to become a dead-serious, hyper-spiritual parent. "Johnny, we've only done four hours of Bible study tonight. We're going to have to make it up tomorrow. Do you have your memory verses down for this week? We've got to be able to say them perfectly before we get to youth group on Wednesday, you know." You'll probably hear kids with parents like that say: "My parents are nuts, and as soon as I'm old enough, I'm out of here." I believe biblical instruction and family devotions are very important, but I also believe it's possible to be so rigid with them that they become counterproductive.

5. *Teachable moments.* "You shall bind them as a sign on your hand. . . . You shall write them on the doorposts of your house." Obedience to the Word of God can't be turned on and off like a switch. The Word is to be ever present in your life so your children understand how constant their obedience must be.

While the fourth resource involves formal, systematic instruction, this tool is much more informal. As your children get older, you should find yourself doing more of this kind of teaching and less of the other. Ideally, they'll begin meeting God on their own, and your interaction with them will be centered more on letting them express what they're learning rather than structuring what they're learning. Instead of leading them in prayer, you'll focus more on praying for each other. Even if their walk with God is not yet as close as you'd like, you can bring God and His Word into the flow of conversations and life circumstances.

A background of systematic instruction lays the foundation for teachable moments. Usually that foundation comes from years of family devotions and Bible study, but as my children got older, I would sometimes assign one of them a book to read or a sermon tape to listen to (with some heavy incentives for completing the assignment) when I saw him or her struggling with a particular issue. That book or tape then became the subject of conversations in the car, at the dinner table, during a break in a driveway basketball game, or whenever. Teachable moments were much easier to come by when we had already established a context, whether over time or with a specific assignment. Teaching became simply a matter of applying truth they had already learned.

Those kinds of situations come up frequently. Watching TV, for example, can be more than a family pastime; it can be an interactive lesson in how to live in an ungodly world. When kids are younger, of course, you focus on the blatant immorality and violence, pointing out how unpleasing to God these things can be. But when they get older, you can go to a deeper level with them. A drama about a guy in a really rough marriage who's drawn to a woman in a rough marriage of her own can turn into a discussion of how Hollywood can play on our sympathies and turn our heart to root for people in an unrighteous relationship. Beyond establishing the lines between what's right and wrong, this kind of teachable moment can train your kids in how those lines get blurred and how a whole culture can fall for such lies. Your children learn to recognize the dynamics of deception and know when they're getting sucked into a false belief system.

The point is that any moment of any day can shape your children's understanding if you're alert to what they're going through and interacting with them regularly about their issues. These opportunities don't need to be forced, as if you're constantly drumming life lessons into your child. They'll come up naturally enough if you're engaged with them in day-to-day life. Ask questions: How did school go? What did you learn today? Who did you spend time with? Talk about what they're learning in class, or the situations their friends find themselves in, or anything else that happens to come up. Children learn to navigate life by

Children learn to navigate life by living it, and if they have a godly guide, they'll learn to navigate well.

living it, and if they have a godly guide to walk them through each day, they'll learn to navigate well.

PREPARE FOR THE OPEN ROAD

Look at this process as similar to teaching your children to drive a car. When they first come home from the hospital, you fasten your babies into a special car seat in the back of the car. They ride in a car seat for several years, and you have to buckle them in tightly and fasten the safety locks every time because they need to know how secure they are. You have total responsibility for your children's safety.

When they get older, your kids can ride in the front seat with you. You still make sure they're buckled in, of course, but they can open the glove compartment, pull out the owner's manual, and flip through it. They can watch how you look both ways before you pull out onto a different street; they can learn to recognize how traffic flows; and they pick up on your sense of safety, courtesy, and discretion. And when you're parked in the driveway, you let them sit in the driver's seat and see how it feels.

As they grow, they can begin to help navigate. They've learned how to read a road map, they've begun studying the driver's ed manual, and they have a good sense of how to get around town. Maybe in an empty parking lot you feel that it's time for them to sit in the driver's seat and practice giving the car a little gas and then tapping the brakes. You let them take a wide turn here and there, put it in reverse, and try to park between the lines. They are learning to handle this big piece of machinery called a car.

One day, they get a permit to drive on the road, as long as you're in the passenger seat. They are in full control of the vehicle, but only under supervision. It's a high degree of responsibility and the last step before driving out in the world on their own, and as white as your knuckles get, you have to let this stage progress. You may hit a few guardrails every once in a while, but that's part of the learning process. You suggest how to do a few things better or how to avoid that near collision next time. You focus on the finer points of driving etiquette, defensive driving, and taking care of oil changes and minor repairs. You're there, but the hands on the wheel are theirs.

And then, after you've done all you can do, they pass the test for their own license, and you hand over the keys for them to try driving on their own. You encourage them by telling them what a great driver they are and how proud you've been as you've watched them learn. The first trip may not be too far from home—it's a huge enough step as it is. But before long, they're driving anywhere and everywhere because they've been training for a long time and because you've gradually prepared them for the responsibility.

At that point, you'll reinforce what you've been teaching them for years: that even though you won't be in that passenger seat anymore, they'll have an invisible counselor named Jesus who's always along for the ride, and they'll need to trust Him to get to their destination safely. He'll know when they're going too fast or when they're about to run out of gas. When they take a wrong turn, He'll help them get back on course. He will do all the things you used to do for them, but now it's their responsibility to listen for His word and heed His instructions.

That's your goal as a parent. You provide your children with the resources of doctrinal truth. You demonstrate your passionate devotion to Christ. You transfer your Bible knowledge into their heart and mind, and you travel with them on the roads you want them to learn. You provide formal times of instruction, and you take advantage of the teachable moments that come up in the natural course of life. The first time they break up with a boyfriend or girlfriend, or when they break an ankle and have to miss the championship game, you're there to teach them how to handle the disappointments of life. When they make the honor roll or lead their team to victory, you're there to celebrate their successes. You teach them how to handle injustice, how to persevere, and how to trust an invisible God. Though you mess up occasionally, miss some opportunities, and are inconsistent at times, you always confess your shortcomings to Jesus and to your family, and you model how to deal with them.

If you do that, you will have done what no school, no amount of money, and no sports or music program can do for them. You will have made eternal deposits in a human heart and given your child an imperishable life. There's no better success for a parent than that.

HOW DO YOU MEASURE SUCCESS?

Think back to that target we talked about in chapter 1. How do you know when you've accomplished your task? If you haven't thought through the plan and know at what point you can give your child the keys, you'll unconsciously focus on activities. "I took him to church, we read the Bible in our home, he was involved in youth group, he's memorized 352 verses. . . ." I've got news for you: A lot of college freshmen and sophomores are rebelling against the faith because their parents were measuring activities and not substance. These kids know a lot of Bible verses and have a long track record of Sunday school lessons and youth group activities, but their parents were missing the target.

When your children transfer their primary love, submission, and dependence from you to Jesus Christ, you will know that they have learned godly obedience.

Here's how you can know when you've hit the target: When your children transfer their primary love, submission, and dependence from you to Jesus Christ, you will know that they have learned godly obedience. Your goal is not to produce independent children; it's to produce children who have transferred their dependence onto the Lord and are growing to become more like Him. Then you've hit the bull's-eye.

> *Parenting Myth: Success as a Christian parent can be measured by how many Bible verses your child has memorized and how often you have family devotions.*

> **Parenting Reality:** You'll know you've succeeded as a Christian parent when your child transfers his or her primary love, submission, and dependence from you to Jesus.

Three noticeable characteristics will be evident in a child who has learned this kind of obedience:

1. *He or she will make wise decisions.* In Philippians 1:9-11, Paul prayed that his spiritual children would be so filled with the knowledge of God and depth of insight that they would be able to discern between good and bad and make decisions that resulted in righteousness. How can your children learn to make good decisions? They need to make a few bad ones along the way. In their midteens, you'll let out the kite string a little, and even if they crash once or twice, they'll eventually learn how to stay aloft.

2. *He or she will keep commitments.* Proverbs 20:6 says, "Many a man claims to have unfailing love, but a faithful man who can find?" Not many people, young or old, will make a commitment and keep it regardless of how inconvenient or difficult it is. Psalm 15 says the godly will not change their minds when they've made an oath that turns out to be to their own detriment. It's a character issue, which can't be measured by how many times a son

or daughter has gone to church. The goal is a strong and pure character, and keeping commitments is a key piece of evidence.

3. *He or she will genuinely care for others.* The litmus test of a follower of Jesus is being winsomely holy and observably loving. Jesus said, "Greater love has no one than this, that one lay down his life for his friends" (John 15:13, NASB). Godliness produces real concern for other people. If a child is self-absorbed, always assuming that the world revolves around what happens in his or her life, that child has not yet learned obedience or transferred trust to the Lord.

When children have learned to make wise decisions, to demonstrate love by keeping their commitments even when that's hard, and to care for other people, they are well on their way to fulfilling God's dream for them. And a parent who has learned to cooperate with God in fulfilling that dream has achieved the ultimate in effectiveness.

Putting It into Practice

Of the five resources discussed in this chapter (doctrinal truth, personal devotion, biblical knowledge, systematic instruction, and teachable moments), which one comes most naturally for you as a parent?

_____

_____

_____

Which one needs the most work?

_____

_____

_____

God's Word says that obedience is your child's greatest responsibility. In contrast, what are some of the things the culture around you says about children and their responsibilities?

_____

_____

_____

What areas of your family's lifestyle need to change to reflect this biblical priority?

_____

_____

_____

Resources

Many resources for doctrinal truth, personal devotion, and biblical knowledge can be found at www.walkthru.org.

To help parents make family devotions brief, biblical, applicable, and fun, consider:

Family Walk (Zondervan, 1991)

For teens:

YouthWalk Devotional Bible (Zondervan, 1997)
YouthWalk magazine (Walk Thru the Bible)

For Bible study and doctrine:

The Daily Walk Bible (Tyndale, 1997)
Closer Walk New Testament (Zondervan, 1990)

5 / How to Discipline Your Child Effectively

Tommy, put those scissors down," you say to your four-year-old.
"No, I don't want to," says Tommy defiantly.

"Do what I tell you. Right now."

"No!"

"I'm going to count to three. One . . . two . . . Tommy, I mean it. Right now. Do you need a time-out?"

Tommy stomps his foot and pouts, refusing to obey. Suddenly, a four-year-old has the upper hand.

"Tommy, I really mean it. One . . . two . . . I don't want to have to spank you."

Your child turns his back and plays deaf. You forcefully take the scissors from his hand—that's the easy part—but getting sharp scissors away from him has now taken a backseat to a larger issue. You told your child to do something and he disobeyed. What's a parent to do?

Or here's another scenario: Your fifteen-year-old breaks curfew, so you take away one of her privileges—no Friday night out with her friends this week. She can't drive yet, so defying you isn't an option unless she sneaks out and catches a ride with someone else. But that's not normally her modus operandi. She's more likely to make your life miserable between now and then—and a few days beyond Friday as well. She ties up the phone for hours, knowing you'll cut her some slack because you're afraid of heaping discipline upon discipline. She keeps her comments short at the dinner table or lets them ooze with poisonous sarcasm. One way or another, she raises the tension level at home until you wish you hadn't been so hard on her simply because she missed a curfew—which is exactly the result she was aiming for.

In both cases, the parent has a problem. It's not an unusual problem; we've all had to deal with it. There's not a responsible parent on the planet who hasn't struggled with getting a child to obey, and it can be an excruciating experience. How do you get your children to mind without losing yours?

That's a challenge, and God's Word has much to say about how we as parents can meet that challenge. It shows us how to provide the kind of discipline that helps our children fulfill their responsibility. If the most important thing for our children to learn is to obey, what do we do when they won't?

Four Parenting Styles

First, it's important to understand how your parenting approach may be contributing to the problem, especially in a culture that has made *discipline* a dirty word. To speak of a parent disciplining a child today evokes images of unreasonable anger and brutal beatings. That's not biblical discipline. Two case studies—one sociological and the other biblical—show us what appropriate, godly discipline is all about.

Sociologist Reuben Hill conducted a study of thousands of teens and parents in Minnesota. Hill put all of his research on a grid with an x-axis, a y-axis, and four quadrants. The horizontal axis (x) measured how much discipline or control parents exercised in their relationship with their child. Zero represented no control—ultra-permissive, "do whatever you want"—and a hundred represented a parental dictatorship—"do what I say, right now; no ifs, ands, or buts." The vertical axis (y) measured love. Zero represented a preoccupied, nonattentive, and nonaffirming parent, and a hundred represented an over-the-top, "I love you so much I can't stop hugging you and everything about you is always wonderful" relationship. Hill found that different parenting styles produced different responses among children.[6]

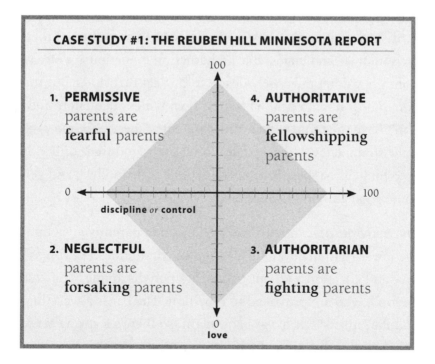

CASE STUDY #1: THE REUBEN HILL MINNESOTA REPORT

100

1. PERMISSIVE
parents are
fearful parents

4. AUTHORITATIVE
parents are
fellowshipping
parents

0 ←——————————→ 100

discipline *or* **control**

2. NEGLECTFUL
parents are
forsaking parents

3. AUTHORITARIAN
parents are
fighting parents

0
love

1. *The Permissive Parent.* The upper left quadrant represents parents who are high in love but low in discipline: the permissive parent. The study revealed that permissive parents tend to produce

children with very low self-esteem and feelings of inferiority. Though the parents express a lot of love, the lack of boundaries leaves their children with a high level of insecurity. The kids feel loved, but they are never sure of their limits. Their parents are generally fearful, afraid of messing up and damaging their children's psyche, so they never set firm boundaries. The kids feel very loved and very unsure of themselves.

2. *The Neglectful Parent.* The lower left quadrant belongs to the worst of all four combinations: the neglectful parent. This kind of parent doesn't express much love and also doesn't really care enough to discipline. Their children tend to grow up with little or no lasting relationship with Mom or Dad. They're estranged because they feel forsaken. The parents' neglect may not necessarily be intentional—they may simply be in the midst of their own traumas and chaos, like an addiction or an abusive situation. They don't purposely desire to neglect their kids, but they don't know how to deal with their own issues adequately and don't have the tools to be healthy parents. These children grow up with unbelievably deep emotional scars, and their only hope is to find Christ, be surrounded by godly role models, and get some good Christian counseling.

3. *The Authoritarian Parent.* The authoritarian parent shows up in the lower right quadrant. This kind of parent doesn't express love and affection well but is very high on discipline. They raise children who are provoked to rebellion. The bar is always high and the "musts" are always abundant, so there's a strong sense of safety. But this kind of parent isn't content just to win the war; they have to win every battle too. Communication between parent and child takes the form of arguing and fighting, especially when the child is old enough to fight back. Authoritarian parents squeeze their kids until the kids can't wait to leave home,

and as soon as they do, they rebel. When Paul told the Ephesians not to overcorrect their children and exasperate them, he was warning authoritarians not to raise children who would reject the faith altogether.

4. *The Authoritative Parent.* Those who land in the upper right quadrant provide the best combination of love and discipline. This kind of parent is authoritative—not an overbearing authoritarian, but a compassionate yet firm authority. They have clear boundaries but are also very loving. I call them "fellowshipping" parents; everyone knows who the boss is, but there's also a connection between parents and child, a consideration that respects and honors who the child is while not compromising his or her disciplinary needs. The result is a child high in self-esteem and equipped with good coping skills.

This secular sociological study found that the parent who balances love and discipline, without compromising either, produces well-adjusted kids who maintain a positive relationship with Mom and Dad. This research, the best available today, affirms parents who express love well and maintain a high degree of control in their home.

> *The parent who balances love and discipline, without compromising either, produces well-adjusted kids who maintain a positive relationship with Mom and Dad.*

All of us want to be in quadrant four, and probably most of us think we are. But before we move on to our biblical case study, consider these questions: Where do you tend to err? If you had to pick a quadrant other than number four to represent your worst moments as a parent, which would it be? Make a mental note of your answer; it will help you later when we look at our parenting through new lenses.

The Spiritual Side of Good Parenting

The second case study I want us to look at doesn't come from sociological research but from inspired Scripture. The subject is a group of spiritual children, Jewish Christians who are rebelling and pulling away from Christ. They are suffering persecution and wondering if the Christian life is worth the trouble. They know the right thing to do—maintain faith in Jesus. But that seems too hard, so they're crossing their arms and turning away.

We can listen in on God's response to these Christians in Hebrews 12:1-11. This is how God disciplines His children. (By the way, any time you see God operating as a parent in Scripture, take note. If you're the kind of parent to your children that God is to His, you're right on target.)

After a brief introduction, the writer of Hebrews reminds his readers that they have "not yet resisted to the point of shedding your blood" in their struggle against sin (v. 4). He also reminds them that God calls them "sons" and encourages them as such (v. 5-6). After all, they're Jewish believers who are very familiar with the Old Testament, so they know the encouragement God has already given in Proverbs 3:11-12: "My son, do not despise the LORD's discipline and do not resent his rebuke, because the LORD disciplines those he loves, as a father the son he delights in." In other words, he acknowledges that they're going through a hard time and suggests they consider whether that hard time is a matter of God's discipline. If it is, it's only because God delights in His children.

Then the writer gets to his main teaching: "Endure hardship as discipline; God is treating you as sons. For what son is not disciplined by his father? If you are not disciplined (and everyone undergoes discipline), then you are illegitimate children and not true sons. Moreover, we have all had human fathers who disciplined us and we respected them for it. How much more should we submit to the Father of our spirits and live!" (vv. 7-9).

The passage gives a very human illustration: "Our fathers disciplined us for a little while as they thought best; but God disciplines us for our good, that we may share in his holiness" (v. 10). The point? "No discipline seems pleasant at the time, but painful. Later on, however, it produces a harvest of righteousness and peace for those who have been trained by it" (v. 11).

Do you see what Scripture is saying here? Far from being a dirty word, discipline is evidence of love. When you consistently discipline your child and do it with the right attitude—compassionately, under control, with consistent boundaries and consequences, and focused on the child's best outcome—you are expressing love exactly as God sometimes expresses His love. It may seem uncomfortable both to you and your child at the time, but in the long run, it's the most selfless, compassionate thing you can do to set your child up for happiness in life and fruitfulness in God's Kingdom.

The Bible's perspective on discipline is affirmed by what many psychologists and sociologists are now learning about child development: that children left to themselves will do what all people left to themselves in a fallen world will do. They'll make bad decisions that produce pain and turmoil in their lives.

"God disciplines us for our good, that we may share in his holiness." (Hebrews 12:10)

Relationships won't work right, money will be mismanaged and debt will pile up, conflict will erupt both within and without, and long-term goals will never be realized. So God tells the Hebrew Christians that the adversity they face comes from His loving hand, not because they're bad, but because He wants the best for them. That's our motivation as parents as well.

If you think that contradicts our culture, you're right. Many books have been written about how harmful discipline can be for children, and they've permeated our thinking. The ideals of permissiveness have been largely discredited lately—even Dr. Benjamin Spock took care in later editions of his best seller *The Common Sense Book of Baby and Child Care* to deal with charges that he advocated permissiveness. He saw the results of an undisciplined upbringing and, in the early 1990s, credited much of society's woes to a lack of "spiritual values." Yet, due in part to his influence, the ideas of permissive parenting still linger in the mind of the average parent.

Five Characteristics of Biblical Discipline

"Discipline" can be a really vague concept, and if you're lost in the landscape of opinions surrounding it out there, you're not alone. If you were to ask a hundred parents to describe their motives and methods of discipline, you might get a hundred different answers. But here's the good news: God's Word is pretty specific about this subject. Since the Bible is always more reliable than opinion surveys—a good principle for any issue in life, by the way—let's take a look at what God says through the writer of Hebrews.

> [4]*In your struggle against sin, you have not yet resisted to the point of shedding your blood.* [5]*And you have forgotten that word of encouragement that addresses you as sons:*
>
> *"My son, do not make light of the Lord's discipline, and do not lose heart when he rebukes you,* [6]*because the Lord disciplines those he loves, and he punishes everyone he accepts as a son."*
>
> [7]*Endure hardship as discipline: God is treating you as sons. For what son is not disciplined by his father?* [8]*If you are not disciplined (and everyone undergoes discipline), then you are illegitimate children and not true sons.* [9]*Moreover, we have all had human fathers who disciplined us and we respected them for it. How much more should we submit to the Father of our spirits and live!* [10]*Our fathers disciplined us for a little while as they thought best; but God disciplines us for our good, that we may share in his holiness.* [11]*No discipline seems pleasant at the time, but painful. Later on,*

however, it produces a harvest of righteousness and peace for those who have been trained by it. (Hebrews 12:4-11)

In this passage, we can discern five distinct characteristics of God's kind of discipline.

1. *The necessity of discipline: to deter destruction (v. 4).* The writer of Hebrews ends chapter 10 with a strong warning coupled with strong encouragement: Those who shrink back from faith and God's will are destroyed, but those who persevere receive all that He has promised. Chapter 11 is full of examples from the men and women in Scripture, and then chapter 12 continues with the encouragement to live a courageous, faithful life. The context of verse 4 is this idea that haphazard living leads to destruction. The message is clear: Disciplined lives reap rewards.

Discipline is about watching your child to see the direction in which he's going. Remember the illustration of giving your child the keys and letting him drive on his own? Action needs to be taken when you see your child take the wrong route and you know he's headed straight for a cliff. You yank the wheel or slam on the brakes, or even put up a barrier so your child won't plunge a thousand feet. He'll get mad for a moment, but ten years down the road he'll thank you.

Discipline—even painful discipline—is actually an expression of love.

Many parents are afraid of making their children mad. I remember the first time one of mine stuck out his lip and said, "I don't love you anymore." My first thought was, "Boy, I don't ever want to be that hard on him again." That's a lot of power to give a five-year-old, isn't it? A better response is to grit your teeth and bear the anger of your child, because it's better to make him frown than let him rush toward destruction. That frown won't last forever. Destruction, however, just might.

Do you see how, from this perspective, discipline—even pain-ful discipline—is actually an expression of love? It always seeks the child's best interest. A mature parent can withstand the anger of their child and say, "That's okay, you don't need to love me right now. You'll love me for it in a few years." It hurts tempo-rarily, but to compromise your child's welfare from fear of losing his love will hurt a lot worse later on.

2. *The means of discipline: actions and words (v. 5).* In the Proverbs 3:11 passage that is quoted in Hebrews, two different Hebrew words are used: *yasar* (discipline), which involves God's actions; and *yakach* (rebuke), which refers to God's words. Hebrews 12:5 tells us not to make light of God's actions and not to lose heart at His words of rebuke. *Yasar* refers to disciplinary actions; *yakach* refers to corrective words.

   As parents, that's exactly how we are to discipline. We bring both words and actions, warnings and consequences, into our children's situations in order to keep them on track.

3. *The motive in discipline: to express love (vv. 6-9).* Not too long after Theresa and I married, as I was trying to finish up my degree at Dallas Seminary, we had another child. What do you do when you've got three young children and are contemplating the topic for your master's thesis? I was so sick of school by that point that I knew I had to choose a topic that would motivate me. Coming from a background in psychology and highly moti-vated to quickly become a good father, I chose (with the obliga-tory long title): "The Role and Responsibility of the Father in Transmitting Values in the Family." I looked at the sociological and psychological literature and empirical studies, and examined the impact a father has in terms of the moral development, sexual identity, and self-image of his children. Then I looked at

the Bible and noted every time a parent showed up in Scripture, cataloged the reference, and compiled the role of a father in the first five books, in the poetic literature, in the Old Testament as a whole, and in the New Testament. Putting the secular research and biblical principles together, I came up with what I considered to be a father's unique role.

The results of all this empirical research blew my mind. For example, when juvenile delinquents, as part of a research study, were asked how they knew their parents' feelings toward them, almost all of them said that lack of discipline in their home was a sign that their parents didn't love them.

One of the most powerful ways to love your child is to be consistent in your discipline.

We often think that we're expressing love when we repeatedly say, "I'll give you another chance." What we're really doing, though, is neglecting to set boundaries that let our children know they're in a safety zone where they can feel secure. One of the most powerful ways to love your child is to be consistent in your discipline. And that's really hard. We're inclined to do whatever we can to maintain a friendship with our kids, when discipline is actually much more important.

I tend to do discipline well for a few weeks, and then find it more convenient to make compromises. Kids pick up on that in an instant. Try listening to them sometime when they aren't aware that a parent can hear them. Their conversation often sounds something like this:

"I got grounded last night."

"Oh no. How long?"

"They said two weeks, but it'll probably just be three or four days."

Where did they get that idea? Children are diligent students of parental behavior. They usually know when they can get away with things. Over time, they learn your breaking points and where you are prone to compromise. They aren't consciously taking notes, of course. They've been taught very well by experience.

4. *The goal of discipline: to teach obedience (v. 9).* When you teach your children godly submission, you're teaching them to do the right thing for the right reason. You want them to get beyond the point where they say "I've got to" and get them to the point of obeying out of love and trust. Their discipline will be primarily external in the beginning, but eventually it should become internal—so integrated into their personality that it's self-discipline rather than imposed discipline. The way you regulate how they speak and act toward other people needs to become a part of who they are so that when you remove the regulations, the behavior remains.

5. *The result of discipline: short-term pain and long-term gain (vv. 10-11).* The reason we don't like to discipline our kids is because it involves short-term pain. We're sympathetic to their feelings, and we never enjoy hurting them. Verse 11 acknowledges the pain, saying *all* discipline—not some or even most, but all— seems not to be pleasant, but painful. But there's a process involved; those who have been trained by it yield the fruit of righteousness.

Someone advised me long ago not to ask myself whether my child liked the discipline I was imposing but to ask whether he would love me when he looked back on the situation years later. That helped me tremendously, especially when one of them would say, "What do you mean I'm grounded? I really can't go? I hate you. You're the worst parent in the world." I even overheard one of my kids, only mildly joking, telling his friends,

"It's like my dad chains me to the bedpost. I never get to go any-where." I would have to remind myself that he was reaping the consequences we had decided on and spelled out up front, and his disobedience produced the expected results. I didn't give in, and my kids came back to me later and said, "Thanks, Dad."

A story from the lives of my twins vividly illustrates this point. Fathers love to pass their skills down to their sons. Some teach their boys to be great mechanics who are handy around the house; others teach them to hunt and fish; and some, like my father, are really good at sports. I grew up knowing virtually nothing about fixing things, but I learned how to hit a baseball and shoot a basketball. I played both sports in high school and then went to college on a basketball scholarship. God even allowed me to play ball overseas for a time after college. So as a dad of two sixth-graders, what did I want them to learn? The same skills I had learned from my dad.

One day the three of us were playing on the floor, and I asked Jason and Eric to show me how many push-ups they could do. Jason could do only one push-up—he was a little chubby at that age—and Eric could do three (mainly because he was so skinny he didn't have as much weight to push as his brother). To me, their inability to do more than a few push-ups meant I was failing them as a father. I envisioned them going into junior high and getting beaten up, so I determined to arm them with strength.

I have to admit that maybe I was just a little overzealous. But at the time, I thought I needed to come up with a game plan. "Okay, guys," I told them. "Set your alarm clock for 6 a.m. tomorrow. We're going to get up and do push-ups and sit-ups every morning for the next three months." Being a morning person, this was not a problem for me. It was a different story for them. But we did it anyway, and I was very enthusiastic about it. When they didn't think they could do another push-up, I'd put my hand under them and make them give me another and another until they completely gave out. They hated it, and at times they hated me.

But after about three weeks, they could do about fifteen push-ups. After three months, they could do about forty. And once they got a taste of success, their motivation increased. A year or so later, they and their friends entered the I've-got-to-be- macho-to-impress-everybody stage that boys often go through, and they started pumping some iron. My son Jason, who could do only one push-up at first, made the football team and went through a weight-training program. Then he became an excellent wrestler and even won his weight class his senior year with a broken hand. At seventeen, he was benching more than 250 pounds, and he'd have to take most of the weights off the bar whenever I'd lift after him because I couldn't come close to lifting what he could.

I watched the level of confidence grow along with my sons' strength and power, all because this father was a bit of a jerk when they were in sixth grade. Discipline, as Hebrews says, is painful for a moment, but it eventually yields fruit. And though few people enjoy the inconvenience and pain of discipline, they look back on the hardship and almost always decide that the fruit was worth the effort.

My experience with my sons is a very physical illustration, but it demonstrates a powerful spiritual truth. It's worth the grief your daughter gives you when you have to tell her that she's too young to date or that she's getting into a relationship that's not good for her. It's worth the groans from your kids when you won't let them watch a movie that everyone else at school got to see, even the Christian kids whose parents weren't quite so uptight about it. It's worth their complaints when you have to limit the amount of time your kids spend on the phone or on the Internet. Knowing how to say no firmly may make them hate you for a moment, but it will make them love you for a lifetime. And you'll have the pleasure of seeing your children experience the peaceful fruit of righteousness.

Stop worrying about being your child's buddy. You are the only one in the world with the primary responsibility of giving your child what he needs, not what he wants. Sometimes that means you have to lay down the law. Afterward you may have to go close yourself up in the bedroom and, with tears in your eyes, tell your spouse how bad you feel for being so hard on your kids. You'll probably need to check yourself occasionally to make sure you're not over the top with your discipline, letting your mate reel you back in if you're getting out of balance. But one way or another, you'll need to enforce the values and biblical principles that God has spelled out in His Word and laid on your heart. You'll need to be firmly convinced that you're preparing your child for a lifetime of fruitfulness. You may not be popular for a moment, but you'll rest easy at night knowing that you're saving your child from a life of destructive habits.

One of the saddest stories in the Bible is of a permissive parent. Eli the priest loved his two sons, Hophni and Phinehas, and rebuked them only mildly for their indiscretions. He was well aware that they stole people's offerings to the Lord to fill their own stomachs and seduced the young women who came to worship in Shiloh. Still, he only told them to stop; he never actually enforced any kind of discipline on them.

If you've read the first few chapters of 1 Samuel, you know the result. God swore to cut off Eli's family forever. On one horrible day, the Israelites were defeated in battle, the Philistines captured the Ark of God, and Hophni and Phinehas were killed. When Eli heard the news, he fell off his chair, broke his neck, and died. It was one of Israel's most devastating moments, all because an old priest wouldn't discipline his sons.

I've always found this story extremely sobering. As much as I want my kids to like me, and as much as I hate conflict in our home, this story rattles me and gives me the backbone to do what's right rather than what's convenient. I'm sure Eli loved his sons; that wasn't the issue. The problem was that his love never translated into discipline and his sons never learned obedience—first not to their father, and therefore not to God. The consequences were tragic. Eli's permissiveness not only destroyed a family, it wounded a nation.

> *Parenting Myth: Your kids will feel most secure if they know you're their buddy.*

> **Parenting Reality:** Your kids will feel most secure if they know you have set appropriate boundaries for them that you aren't afraid to enforce.

You have higher ambitions for your children, don't you? You want them to grow up bearing the fruit of righteousness, which always leads to lasting joy. That's why it's absolutely imperative to learn how to say no. Be willing to let your children get mad at you from time to time. Keep your eyes on their ultimate welfare instead of on their momentary comfort. Effective parenting always requires effective discipline.

Be willing to let your children get mad at you from time to time.

You probably struggle with what that discipline should look like. I certainly did. How do you know when it's too harsh, or when it's not harsh enough? How do you know when you're disciplining a child for his own welfare and when you're punishing him out of your own frustration? The difference between discipline and punishment may seem subtle in your own experience, but from God's perspective, it's a monumental distinction. As we get into the nuts and bolts of discipline in the next chapter, you'll see how His perspective can answer those questions.

Putting It into Practice

Ask your spouse and/or a good friend—people who can be completely honest with you—to examine Reuben Hill's analysis of the four styles of parenting (see page 85). Then ask them to describe where you fit on the grid and to give some examples that support their opinion. (For some of us, it may be hard not to get defensive, but try to listen with an open mind.) Does your perception of your parenting line up with what your spouse/friends have told you? If you believe change in your parenting style is needed, how might you adjust your style to best suit the emotional needs of your children?

_____

_____

_____

_____

_____

_____

_____

6 / Punishment versus Discipline

Mark's teeth were clenched and the veins in his neck were bulging. His son, Chad, had skipped school again—the fifth time in the last two months. Somehow, Chad and his buddies figured a few days of surfing were more worthwhile than an entire semester's worth of grades. So whenever the wave reports were favorable, they'd meet off campus, drive down to the beach together, and return home about fifteen minutes after school was out, hoping their parents would never discover their adventure—but clearly not too worried if they did. And they almost always did. Today, after getting a call from the principal and smelling the lingering scent of saltwater on his son, Mark was at the end of his patience.

"Chad, I can't believe you did it again!" Mark yelled. "How many times have we had this conversation? You're in so much trouble. . . ." At a loss for words, Mark's mind searched for a punishment that would be severe enough. He felt betrayed by the son who had promised him two weeks earlier that this would never happen again. He was so mad that all he could think about was payback.

That's an understandable emotion for a frustrated parent to have, but when action flows out of that emotion, parenting has taken a turn for the worse. That dynamic will eventually render your efforts to raise godly children ineffective, and

Punishment produces a child laden with guilt and determined to get out from under it.

here's why: The idea of punishment implies repaying someone with what he or she deserves. That's the antithesis of the gospel. Punishment produces a child laden with guilt and determined to get out from under it, and Christlikeness is never the result. An effective parent has to learn the difference between punishment and discipline.

	PUNISHMENT	DISCIPLINE
Purpose	To inflict penalty for an offense	To train for correction and maturity
Focus	Past misdeeds	Future correct acts
Attitude	Hostility and frustration on the part of the parent	Love and concern on the part of the parent
Resulting emotion in the child	Fear and guilt	Security

As you can see, although the actions parents take to correct their children may look the same, understanding the difference between discipline and punishment makes all the difference in the world in terms of attitude and results. Allow me to take a brief look at the theological background behind these concepts to help you grasp how understanding this difference can transform your approach to your child's misbehavior.

The Gospel of Grace

We love the gospel of grace when we come to God with our sins. None of us wants justice in the sense of God giving us what we deserve. But as much as we love His mercy when applied to us, we have a really hard time applying it to others—especially when the "other" is someone who can wound our hearts as deeply as our child can. The closer the relationship, the more betrayed and frustrated we feel. And those kinds of feelings can lead to ill-conceived punishments.

Understanding the difference between discipline and punishment can transform your approach to your child's misbehavior.

Think about how God disciplines. Some translations of Hebrews 12:6, where the writer quotes Proverbs to demonstrate that God disciplines His children, use an inadequate word: "he *punishes* everyone he accepts as a son" (italics added). The translation itself isn't wrong, but it doesn't capture the full meaning of the word. Literally, it means to forcefully correct, to scourge, to take whatever drastic measure is necessary to get someone to obey. Punishment, when not clarified in English with a fuller definition, implies retribution. It can be entirely a matter of payback.

As you know, that's not the gospel. When we've put our faith in Jesus, God doesn't punish us for what we did. The focus of punishment is always past tense: "First you did this, then you did this, and now you have to pay the price." In His mercy, God wiped away all eternal, spiritual implications of our pasts; He doesn't treat His children according to the rules of punishment.

Very simply, the gospel is that God became a man, came to earth, lived a perfect life, died on a cross to pay for the sins of all mankind, rose again from the dead on the third day, and was seen by over five hundred witnesses. Those who want that redemption applied to themselves must understand that we have a sin problem—we've all violated the commands of a holy God—and that there's no way to the Father except through the Son. Salvation means receiving the gift of Jesus' work on the Cross.

When we do that, the Spirit of God enters our lives, we are born again, and the Spirit dwelling in us now begins to develop the life of Christ in us. God's wrath toward sin was spent on Jesus as the Son hung on a symbol of the curse. When Jesus said, "My God, my God, why have you forsaken me?" (Mark 15:34), He was experiencing the full wrath of God for all the sins of all mankind for all of history. He was the propitiation for us—in our place, He absorbed God's anger toward human sinfulness. Sharing the gospel isn't about convincing people to believe a doctrine and live better; it's about letting people know the really good news that we've been forgiven. All one needs to do to receive that salvation is turn from wickedness and receive Christ's gift.

What does all this have to do with parenting? If Jesus took all the punishment for you and me, He also took all of it for our children. I don't want to teach my kids that I need to pay them back for the bad things they've done. I want them to understand that the only way to make right what they did is to trust that when Jesus died on the cross, He paid for their sins. It makes no sense for me to fellowship with God on the basis of mercy and with my children on the basis of judgment. Since Jesus took the punishment, my role as a parent is not to punish them. My role is to provide appropriate consequences and instruction to help them see how their behavior displeases God and to teach them how to cooperate with God's work in their lives. The Bible calls this discipline.

Punishment produces some very negative characteristics in your children: guilt, shame, bitterness, resentment, regret, self-pity, fear, and more. Because it's focused on the past, children feel helpless. They can't undo what they've already done, and they can't change the circumstances that their behavior has produced. Punishment doesn't give them a means to right their wrongs; the tools they need to understand redemption aren't included in the punishment package. It is simply retribution that leads to a lot of negative emotions.

Discipline, on the other hand, is future-focused, always pointing toward future acts. It has nothing to do with retribution and everything to do with redemption. Whereas the purpose of punishment is to inflict a penalty for an offense, the purpose of discipline is to train for correction and maturity. Whereas the origin of punishment is the frustration of the parent, the origin of discipline is a high motivation for the welfare of the child. And whereas the result of punishment is fear and shame, the result of discipline is security. Discipline *always* holds the child's best interests, not the parent's anger, in the forefront. It is never out of control.

> *It makes no sense for me to fellowship with God on the basis of mercy and with my children on the basis of judgment.*

> *Parenting Myth: Discipline requires parents to penalize their child as payback for an offense.*

> **Parenting Reality:** Discipline means applying appropriate consequences to encourage a child to make better choices in the future.

What messages are you sending your kids? Few parents will bluntly declare that they're penalizing a child for his misbehavior. We don't express punishment in terms of vengeance. But when the veins are popping, the voice is escalating, and the parent towers intimidatingly over their children, the message is easily confused. You may have discipline in mind, but your children probably interpret your outbursts of anger as pure punishment. It needs to be clear in their minds that you are imposing boundaries for their good because you love them.

There will be times, of course, when you are angry. Just because you don't discipline out of anger doesn't mean you won't feel angry. My kids have done things that made me livid, and it took me between ten minutes and an entire day to calm down. But I've learned that I am not ready to discipline my child until I can do so under control. The best way to do that is to have your child go to his room, or for you to go to your room, or both. There's nothing wrong with taking time to invite God to "clothe" you in the Spirit of Christ, remind yourself that Jesus has already paid for your children's sins, ask God to help you handle your anger appropriately, and then deal with the situation rationally. It's fine to tell your children how upset you are, but the focus soon needs to turn to helping them get right with God and learn how to correct the behavior for the future. I confess that this approach takes a lot more work on the parent's part, and a lot more self-control. But in our home and countless others, it has turned the disciplining process from an ugly exchange of hurtful emotions to a time of resolution and deeper intimacy between parent and child.

> *Discipline has nothing to do with retribution and everything to do with redemption.*

Now that we've talked about the "why" behind disciplining our children, let's look at what Scripture says about the "how."

Action = Consistent Consequences

You may have noticed that discipline is a fairly controversial topic in our day. If you watch a news digest program regularly, you'll eventually see a story that somehow involves spanking—either about someone who was abused as a child or someone who is in trouble for abusing their children. The subject is almost always treated with suspicion or even horror, as though anyone who spanks a child is unenlightened and barbaric. It is rarely presented as rational and frequently portrayed in its extremes. And yet the Bible, which quite a few of us still believe is true, says things like "Do not spare the rod." How are we to sort out the controversy and be obedient to God?

Actions and words—it all goes back to those two Hebrew words, *yasar* and *yakach*.[6] The concept of *yasar* is chastisement, and it almost always implies something physical. Proverbs 13:24 is clear: "He who spares the rod hates his son, but he who loves him is careful to discipline him." It doesn't say the one who spares the rod has the wrong opinion about discipline, it says he *hates* his son. Proverbs 22:15 is also clear: "Folly is bound up in the heart of a child, but the rod of discipline will drive it far from him." A lot of people may not like those verses, but the Bible doesn't really give us the option of picking our favorites and ignoring the ones we don't like. These are part of the inspired Word of God, and we have to approach them that way.

Though spanking is controversial, I would suggest that there are, in fact, times when it's appropriate to spank your kids. I understand that for some parents, that's hard; discipline is not for the faint of heart. You don't need to spank very often, especially if you do it properly and early in their lives, but God seems to have made children with a little extra fatty tissue in certain areas of their bodies where a firm swat does no damage. At certain ages and in certain circumstances, spanking is the most effective—and compassionate— approach you can take.

"Folly is bound up in the heart of a child, but the rod of discipline will drive it far from him." (Proverbs 22:15)

For example, you may have told your nine-year-old son that you don't want him hanging out at the home of the kid who lives three doors down. You know the parents are often away and that alcohol is available and guns aren't locked away. Say that God graciously ordains, as He often does for parents, that you drive by at the exact moment your son is coming out of the front door of that house. You make it very clear to your son that if he ever does that again, there will be an uncomfortable consequence, and he knows exactly what you mean when you say that. A couple of days later, you drive by and see him coming out of that house again. What do you do?

You have to follow through on your word and impose the expected consequence. Children go through various phases of rebellious attitudes, such as talking back, lying, and stealing, and even though they know where the boundaries are, they'll cross them to see what happens. At certain stages of their development, that's how they ask that question we discussed back in chapter 3 about how secure they are. When we as parents fail to follow up consistently with firm, concrete discipline, it makes our children very insecure.

In one way or another, every child will fight this battle with his parent. The earlier you win that battle, the better, both for your sanity and your child's. You can win it when your kids are toddlers, or you can wait and try to win it when they're teenagers. Victory comes a lot easier when a child is two, and it's more quickly accomplished at that age when you use spanking, appropriately and lovingly applied, to enforce it.

Using "battle" terminology when talking about discipline may seem harsh to some, but from all the psychological research I've done, a clear and controlled spanking is far less damaging to a child than the repeated yelling and screaming a lot of parents go through. It's also far less damaging than the ambiguous boundaries and mixed messages a lot of parents give their children. When a child knows he's done something wrong—something that is clearly forbidden—and is spanked for that wrong, shown love, prayed with, restored, and allowed to proceed with a clean conscience, he experiences much less trauma than the child whose parents don't know how to enforce discipline.

In contrast, when a child is sent to her room for a time-out, the measure of discipline is more protracted. The message usually isn't as clear, the resolution is often more uncertain, and the opportunity to cleanse the conscience isn't immediate. There's less sense of closure. Sometimes it may be a good first consequence when verbal instructions are ignored—I don't encourage spanking as a necessary first resort in every situation, since a loss of privileges or a time- out can often get your point across—but I don't believe parents should be afraid of applying physical punishment in a godly way. The idea ingrained in some people that time-outs are always better than spankings is a false assumption.

I want to be very clear that discipline never involves slapping or hitting a child. Anyone who has a problem with this needs to get help immediately. If you come from an abusive background, the last thing you want to do is continue the cycle with your children. If that is your situation, let me strongly encourage you to swallow your pride, override your fear, and do whatever it takes to protect your kids from physical abuse. Also, remember it's never appropriate to spank babies or toddlers younger than fifteen to eighteen months of age. Even shaking a very young child can lead to brain damage or death.

Spanking—not slapping or hitting—should always be done by a parent who is in control of his or her emotions. In our home, we used a wooden spoon to spank. My kids dreaded seeing the wooden spoon coming, but they never had to dread the hand of Mom or Dad. Our hands were used exclusively for loving touches, caresses, and hugs; an inanimate spoon was the object of discipline. That may seem like hairsplitting to some, but I believe that in the psyche of the child, there's a tremendous difference. Scripture makes a strong case for the use of appropriate spanking, and it also identifies an object (the rod) as the tool. Some may believe that the rod implies discipline of any kind. All I know is that using an object fits with biblical instruction, and I'm much more comfortable reserving my hands for loving touches. Regardless of the method, the Bible's word on discipline clearly demands that parents be responsible and diligent in spanking, but strongly prohibits physical abuse of any kind. Obviously, the biblical approach is balanced, reasonable, and controlled. So let's get very practical. What does it look like to spank in a way that obeys Scripture, modifies attitudes and behavior, and actually strengthens the bond between parent and child?

Seven Steps

Don't panic when you have to use action to enforce discipline. I know how much second-guessing a parent can do. Let me give you seven key steps that will enable you to discipline your child without fear of overstepping your bounds.

1. *Clear warning.* Your first interaction with your child about a situation should be verbal. A child should never be blindsided by the discipline you hand down to her. It should always be preceded by a clear warning, both for her sake and for yours. You want to know whether your child deliberately crossed a line or made an honest mistake. A clear warning will help her steer clear of danger and will help you know you're correcting intentional disobedience. That's why it would be appropriate to issue a warning to Johnny the first time you see him walking out of the neighbor boy's house.

   A child should never be blindsided by the discipline you hand down to her.

   The enforcement of discipline comes only after words have not done the job. Physical means of correction are only appropriate in cases of clear disobedience, and then only at certain ages.

2. *Establish responsibility.* It's important for your child to own up to his misbehavior. Many parents make the mistake of asking,

"Why did you do that?" That's not a good question; "why" doesn't help him admit his responsibility in the situation. Besides being a theological no-brainer—your child is a sinner with a predisposition to disobedience, which he inherited from you and every other generation all the way back to the first parents in the Garden—that question gives him room to inject shades of gray into his understanding and explanations. He'll begin to rationalize, and you'll lose sight of the real issue. Here's a better way to go about it:

"Johnny, *what* did you do wrong?"

"Nothing. Everyone was going over to that house, and I just went in for a minute."

"Try again. What did you do wrong?"

"I only went in to . . ."

"I'm going to give you one more chance. What did we talk about?"

"I'm not supposed to go over there for any reason."

"So *what* did you do wrong?"

"I disobeyed you."

Do you see how, with that kind of conversation, you're calm, controlled, and not trying to punish? You're trying to help him learn. Remember that your child *can't* learn without being able to own up to his responsibility. No one can. When you put your child in a position of having to do that, you're preparing him for responsible adulthood.

Remember to always keep your focus on the child's behavior, not his identity. If Johnny says, "I'm a bad person" or "You don't like me anymore," affirm how much he is loved and how special he is, but turn his attention immediately back to his actions. You want him to understand that the act was wrong and that he is fully capable of doing the right thing.

3. *Avoid embarrassment.* Never embarrass your children in front of their friends, siblings, or even strangers. Don't yank them out of

a booth at a restaurant, don't yell where everyone around can hear you, or do anything else that will make your children feel as if all eyes are on them. All that accomplishes is shame. Instead, go to a private place. At home, that can be the bedroom. In public, it can be a trip to the restroom for a young child or a firm statement that "we need to talk later" to an older child. However you do it, don't damage your kids' esteem among their peers or even among strangers. Embarrassment can do a lot of damage that you'll have a hard time undoing later on.

4. *Communicate grief.* I want my children to know that more than being angry, I'm disappointed and heartbroken when they disobey. Early on in their lives, I let them know I trusted them. And when that trust has been violated, they need to know that the relationship is wounded. Many times I've had tears roll down my face when their actions hurt me and betrayed our relationship. When kids see the grief of their parents, they'll better understand how their sin affects God. They'll understand that God isn't shaking His fist at us every time we make a mistake, but He grieves just as a loving parent does when witnessing the destructive nature of disobedience.

5. *Flick your wrist.* This is an extremely practical method that will save you a lot of second-guessing. Remember the point of a spanking: It's to sting, to provide a painful deterrent to misbehavior, not to injure.

A few years ago there was a legal showdown between a church and the city of Atlanta over the right to physically beat children. The pastor insisted, contrary to Scripture, that the repeated, harsh beatings practiced by families in the church were mandated by God. The belief of this church was that God's rod was severe and should be used in full force.

The Bible never implies that the rod of discipline should be violent. It offers no specifics about how hard a spanking should be, and there's no reason to assume that it's talking about a brutal form of punishment. Just the opposite, in fact. A parent who reaches back and swings hard is acting out of anger and frustration, not out of love and desire for the child's welfare. That's unbiblical by anyone's definition.

When you spank, use a wooden spoon or some other appropriately sized paddle and flick your wrist. That's all the force you need. It ought to hurt—an especially difficult goal for mothers to accept—and it's okay if it produces a few tears and sniffles. If it doesn't hurt, it isn't really discipline, and ultimately it isn't very loving because it will not be effective in modifying the child's behavior. As James Dobson has wisely said, "our objective . . . is not simply to shape the will, but to do so without breaking the spirit."[7] Have the child lean over his bed and make sure you apply the discipline with a quick flick of the wrist to the fatty tissue of the buttocks, where a sting can occur without doing any damage to the body. You want to be calm, in control, and focused as you firmly spank your child, being very careful to respect his body.

As your children get older and begin to think more abstractly, spanking becomes less effective and less necessary. My wife knew one of our sons was too old for a spanking when she applied her flick of the wrist and he just turned around, looked at her, and laughed. A preteen is probably getting past the spanking stage and more into the lost-privilege approach. But if you've done your job earlier in their lives, spanking will have become less necessary at that point anyway. A firm, grace-controlled hand of discipline in early years, combined with a loving attitude, will usually prevent or soften the rebellion of later years.

6. *Sincere repentance.* When my kids were small, I'd let them sit in my lap after a spanking and cry for a while. That was a great time

to model for them the love behind the discipline. Then after a few minutes, I'd ask, "Are you ready to talk about this with Daddy and with God?" When I received a nod and could tell repentance and genuine sorrow had occurred, I revisited the issue and asked them, "What did you do wrong?" I wanted to help them clearly relate the discipline to the behavior, not to them as a person. Then I would ask, "With whom do you need to make things right?" Often they would realize they needed to make things right not just with me and with God, but also to apologize to a brother or sister. Then I'd take the opportunity to coach them in how to approach God, what to say, how to confess their sin, and how to receive forgiveness. When they said something like, "I'm sorry, God, for _____. Please forgive me," I would tell them how special they were, both to me and to God, and that they'd been disciplined to correct misbehavior, not because they were a bad person. Those dialogues trained them for a life of relating to God humbly and honestly as no other experience could. And in later years my children told me that some of the times they'd felt closest to me were during those periods of forgiveness and reconciliation.

7. *Unconditional love.* For my part, some of the most intimate, touching moments I ever had with my kids were right after exercising discipline. So after disciplining your child, let me encourage you to take him in your arms and pray, "Thank you, Lord, for my precious boy, for the wonderful way You've made him, for the amazing guy he is, and for all the gifts You've given him. Please help him remember what's right and give him the strength to do it. Thank You that he has taken responsibility for what he did. We know You've taken a big eraser and wiped it off the board. You've forgiven him and made him absolutely clean, and I forgive him too." Then give him a big hug and go do something

fun. He'll know he's still accepted and that there's absolutely no barrier between the two of you.

The picture and the process I've just described don't fit the portrayal of spanking that our culture tries to give us, do they? A parent who disciplines his child this way is not an angry, insensitive person with a big club and a vicious agenda. Instead, this is a picture of using the rod God's way to bring about actions that will keep a child from destruction. That's about as loving and compassionate as a parent can get.

It Works

As I've taught this material live and through our small-group curriculum on DVD, I've been amazed by the positive feedback not only in the United States, but also from places as far north as Russia and as far south as South Africa. The feedback from parents reminds me that God's Word transcends culture and makes a radical difference in children's lives.

Recently I received an e-mail from a woman who had attended one of our "Effective Parenting" seminars:

> I've been exhausted by the confrontation and the drama that's often associated with disciplining, but your message was the kick in the pants that I needed to do what was right before God and to be more loving to my son. Thank you.
>
> This morning during our time of school, his attitude really stunk. He was argumentative and disobedient, he was clearly challenging my authority, and then he began to pick on his little brother.
>
> Well, we did what you said. We went upstairs, went through the process, and two quick stings later he was sobbing and repenting in my arms and apologizing. I held him, and then he said, "Mama, I'm sure glad they made

wooden spoons." We prayed and he snuggled back into my arms, the rest of our day has been peaceful, without the arguments and disobedience we've been experiencing recently. Thank you for the reminder I needed to return to the courage to discipline.

Lest you think this story is simply anecdotal evidence to make a point, consider some of the recent secular psychological research that supports spanking as an effective and viable means of discipline. In the Santa Cruz newspaper—which, by the way, represents one of the most liberal communities in the United States—I read anarticle with the headline, "Study: Childhood Spanking Leaves No Permanent Scars."[8] The text of the article spelled it out: "Occasional mild spanking of young children will not create any lasting harm that is carried into adolescence, according to a study released Friday. Such discipline does not hurt youngsters' social or emotional development, the researchers reported. The study was being presented at a meeting in San Francisco of the American Psychological Association."

Many people have bought into a bad, stereotypical model of spanking, where out-of-control parents and religious fanatics beat children instead of disciplining them. Not surprisingly, they have rejected it entirely, assuming that since they don't know how to do it right, it shouldn't be done at all. "Extreme spanking" has dominated the discussion at the expense of more moderate practices of physical discipline. As a result, a huge segment of the population believes spanking is barbaric, basing that opinion on the abuses rather than the biblical model. But many parents who believe this are having enormous problems at home—constant conflict, high tension, complete loss of control, and no tools to deal with any of it.

If you're consistent with the actions of discipline for a few weeks, you'll find that your children have clear boundaries, and they're likely to have a clearer conscience and changed behavior. You'll probably sense much less destructive stress in your home environment as well. Your children will feel a lot more loved, and they'll have the privilege and blessing of being in a home that's at peace.

Putting It into Practice

If you are uncomfortable using biblical spanking as a form of discipline, identify the reasons why. (Check all that apply.)

___ Lack of belief in spanking
___ Unable to manage frustration/anger and portray love/gentleness while spanking
___ Too softhearted to inflict pain on my child
___ Too difficult to spank consistently
___ Other_____

What are some instances when you would consider using spanking as a form of discipline? For example: "When my child deliberately defies me," "When Jeffrey talks back disrespectfully and intentionally," "Only when I have given clear warning first."

SCENARIOS	SITUATIONS	STIPULATIONS
_____	_____	_____
_____	_____	_____
_____	_____	_____
_____	_____	_____
_____	_____	_____
_____	_____	_____
_____	_____	_____

In contrast, what are some examples of situations in which you would use other forms of correction? For example: "For minor infractions"; "When Jeffrey forgets to answer properly, I will correct him verbally"; "When another consequence is more logical" such as taking away a privilege to correct misuse of that privilege.

SCENARIOS	SITUATIONS	STIPULATIONS

7 / Words That Discipline

In the last chapter, we looked at the Hebrew word *yasar*—correction using consistent actions to deter bad behavior. That word focuses on "the rod" that reproves a child and helps him or her walk with God and be obedient.

This chapter is about the *yakach*—correction using words. Proverbs 3:11-12 tells us also not to despise the Lord's rebuke, His words of correction and reproof. In this chapter I want to highlight the part that words can play in discipline because, to be honest, you normally don't need to spank very often if you start early and do it consistently. That practice will make the boundaries clear in a child's mind, and he won't spend years testing them over and over again because he'll know where they are. Clarity at the front end of a child's development can actually save him and you much of the more painful discipline later on.

You may not always know exactly what to say to your kids when they need your verbal discipline. Many parents have a clear idea of how they want their children to behave but unknowingly use words that actually undermine their ability to accomplish that goal. In this chapter, I'd like to share some specific ways you can use words more effectively to correct your child.

Say No Firmly

Has this scene ever played out in your house?

Child: "Mom, a few of us want to go to this movie. I know it's R-rated, but I've heard it's really clean, and I think it's going to be okay. Please?"

Parent, who has seen the preview and knows what it will be like: "Oh, honey, I don't think so."

Child: "Please, Mom? I just *have* to go. Everybody's going. I'll shut my eyes during the parts that are really bad."

Parent, using a wishy-washy tone of voice that leaves the possibility open: "I don't feel good about it."

Child: "Don't you trust me? I mean, I'm fifteen years old. I'm going to be old enough to go on my own soon enough."

Before you know it, you've drifted down a trail of rationalizations, and the confrontation is going to get ugly. Why? You didn't say no firmly.

As soon as you say something ambiguous, like "I don't know" or "I don't feel very good about it," you're telling your children that they have some wiggle room in which to maneuver. You've opened a door that practically invites them to try to sway you. When little Jacob picks a toy off the shelf and asks, "Can we get it? Pleeeeease?" and you say, "Oh, I don't think so," even at his young age, he knows there's still a possibility you'll give in. Small children will try to beg you until you relent; older ones will come up with some of the most creative rationalizations you've ever heard until you're tired of thinking up good rebuttals.

A firm no will eliminate a lot of the anxiety both you and your child have about the situation. In the example above of the teenager and the movie, if you know in your heart that it's the wrong movie and the wrong crowd, just say, "I'm sorry, honey. Absolutely not. That's not a good movie because it doesn't have the kinds of things I want going into your mind."

"I don't understand why not," a disappointed teenager often responds.

"Honey, I'm glad you asked that. Let's sit down and talk about it." And you can take the opportunity to reaffirm your love for her, acknowledge that it means a lot to her and that there's a lot of pressure on her to do certain things with her friends, and guide her to think through the situation as a Christian should. If at all possible, open the Scriptures in a nonlegalistic way and show her some verses that will help her understand that your decision isn't backed up by "because I said so," but grows out of God's deepest desires for our well-being. Romans 12:2, for example, emphasizes the benefits of avoiding worldly behavior: "Do not conform any longer to the pattern of this world, but be transformed by the renewing of your mind. Then you will be able to test and approve what God's will is—his good, pleasing and perfect will." Proverbs 13:20 points out the consequences God wants to spare us from as well as the benefit of God's favor: "He who walks with the wise grows wise, but a companion of fools suffers harm." Explain why you said no and that the rules have a heart of love behind them—God's heart and yours. Your tone of voice can make all the difference. You can help her see God's commands not as restrictions against fun, but as guardrails of protection to ensure her best—His good and acceptable will in her life.

I believe about 80 percent of your need to discipline will be eliminated if you learn to say what you mean and mean what you say. Children are much less likely to pester a parent with repeated requests if the parent is decisive.

If you really aren't sure of your answer when your kids make a request, don't give a firm no. Tell your child that you need to pray about it and, if applicable, talk about it with your mate. Promise to give her an answer the next day. And when you give that answer, be firm about it.

I believe about 80 percent of your need to discipline will be eliminated if you learn to say what you mean and mean what you say.

By the way, in such situations, I've discovered a powerful way to help your child be a part of the process and develop her own convictions at the same time. While you're considering her request, give your child this assignment: "Why don't you spend some time praying about it? Ask God what He would have you do, and tell me tomorrow what you think He is saying." That's letting the string out on the kite a little more. It doesn't automatically set you up as the bad guy, and it helps deepen your child's relationship with God. True, some kids will say a quick prayer and come back with the same plea the next day. But you'd be surprised how often a child will change her mind once God is personally brought into the situation. I can remember several times when I thought through a request and had about decided that I'd give permission, only to have my child come back and say, "You know, I don't think the Lord wants me to go."

When that happens, you can know that the process of transferring trust from you to God is well under way. You can act as a priest, a go-between, in your child's relationship with God only to a certain point. Eventually, he or she will need to be able to hear God's voice and obey without your prodding.

Use Contracts

When kids get into preteen and teen years, power struggles escalate. God has wired them to stretch their wings and prepare themselves to fly out of the nest. They push for more and more independence. Meanwhile, you're still their authority, and you still have the responsibility to make sure they learn obedience and are protected from life-threatening crashes. It's a process with a lot of tension in it.

One way to reduce some of that tension is to use contracts to spell out the consequences you and your child agree to abide by should he violate a particular standard you have set. When we are the authority all the time, we never really transfer trust to our children. We put ourselves in a position of being the heavy hand that is always pushing them down and keeping them dependent—at least that's how they will perceive us. By making a contract that addresses the issues that are most contentious, you can transfer a lot of the responsibility to them. When the contract is violated, you can point out that the issue was their responsibility; they didn't live up to their agreement. When executed properly, your child won't feel oppressed; he'll realize he's the one who blew it.

So how do you set contracts that work? The best way is to pick four or five of your biggest power struggles—those areas where you bump heads most often, whether it be over chores, schoolwork, phone privileges, talking back, or how they treat their siblings. There are a million possibilities, but you will probably think of the big ones right away. Then describe the behaviors that cause conflict on the left side of a sheet of paper. Next take some time to pray and maybe even fast for a meal or two to be sure your attitude is right before sitting down with your child to talk.

"Every week we argue about [fill in the blank], and we're both tired of the stress, right? I don't like being upset with you, nagging, and losing my cool, and I'm pretty sure you don't like it either. I love you too much to be in constant conflict with you. Here are the things that seem to be a source of conflict. I am commanded by God to help you learn to obey, and since I have not been very effective in doing that so far, why don't we agree on what the consequences should be if you don't do your part in these things? I want you to tell me what consequences would motivate you to do what you know is right."

Then go through them one by one. "You've been picking on your brother and being sarcastic to everyone in the house. What would help you obey in this area? You tell me."

"Well, if I had to miss the next basketball game, that would get me to watch what I say."

"Okay, I'll agree to that." And you let him or her write the consequence on the line corresponding to the behavior on the right side of the paper.

BEHAVIOR:	CONSEQUENCES:
1. Failure to clean my room	no video games for 5 days
2. Miss curfew	forfeit use of car for 1 week

Many parents roll their eyes when they think about letting their kids help determine the consequences for their actions, assuming that a child will choose something easy and painless. You'd be surprised. Most often, the child's idea of an appropriate consequence is much harsher than yours. The point simply is to take seriously your child's recommendations and come up with appropriate consequences you both can agree upon.

I did this with one of my sons who had worked hard to earn a first-team spot on the basketball squad. He finally did make the first team and couldn't wait for the big game when he would get to start. Long before, however, we had made a contract on an issue on which it was perpetually difficult for him to obey. The contract said that if he disobeyed, he'd have to miss two days of practice, which would mean he couldn't start in the game that week.

What do you think he said to me after he disobeyed the week before the big game? "Dad, you can't do this to me! I've worked all season for this. I *have* to be there for practice or I'll lose my spot. What are you trying to do to me?"

"Wait just a minute. What do you mean, 'What am I doing to you?' " And I pulled out the contract that had both our signatures on it. "We agreed that this behavior would be followed by that consequence, right? I didn't do this to you. You did this to yourself."

Do you see how that lets out the string a little more? He's responsible for both his decisions and the consequences. This process forces our children to take personal responsibility for their behavior. Now instead of being the nagging, negative parent who wouldn't let him do this or that, I could actually sympathize with him; I'd seen how hard he worked to start in that game. I was bummed out too. I told him that I was on his side, and I offered to help explain the situation to the coach. But I had to let him experience the results of his behavior, which he had agreed to beforehand.

Contracts work very effectively from about age eleven or twelve on up, depending on the maturity and personality of your child. The words of an agreement can allow you to sit on the same side of the conflict with your children while letting their own actions enforce the discipline. You can cry with them, encourage them, and support them without ever compromising the agreement. You are no longer the bad guy; you are a companion in their struggle against disobedience. The key to making contracts and other forms of verbal discipline effective is the wise implementation of consequences.

Use Consequences

When you're in a really difficult situation with a child who seems completely out of control, you need to have a plan. Many parents say to me, "I don't know what to do. She didn't come home last night, everything's chaos in our house, and I'm powerless to do anything about it." Sometimes in a parenting crisis we are so close to the situation that we can't see the obvious, so I often ask a few diagnostic questions: "Whose car is she driving? Who's paying for the gas that goes in the car? What about her insurance? Whose room is she sleeping in? Who's buying her food?" And so on. The answers almost always reveal that the parent is not even close to being "powerless." They're just unaware of or afraid to use the power they have.

> *Parenting Myth: You don't have much leverage with a teen who is completely out of control.*
>
> **Parenting Reality:** You probably have much more leverage than you realize.

If you have a child who is way past the age of spanking and openly defiant to your authority, you probably have quite a bit more leverage than you think. Take the car keys back and cut off the money supply, for starters. Having responsibility requires being responsible, and if your child can't demonstrate what it means to be responsible, then the privileges that go along with responsibility need to be taken away. Once she's been able to demonstrate responsible behavior, she can have the privileges back. Until then, that's the way it is.

You need to use words to clearly spell out consequences ahead of time—what behaviors would violate your rules, how and when the consequences would be enforced, and exactly what the consequences are. And then you need to resolutely make sure you apply the consequences; otherwise, your words will eventually become meaningless.

I shared earlier about one of my sons who was giving us all kinds of problems during his teens. He loved us as people but was utterly frustrated by our standards as parents. Christianity, in his own words, really cramped his style. He refused to comply with the household rules and was determined to live his way on his terms. This went on for about four years. Finally, we had one of the most difficult conversations I've ever had to have. I had tried every form of discipline described in this book. I spent time with him, prayed for him, and practiced tough love, but nothing changed his clearly unacceptable attitudes and actions.

As we sat in the car in front of our house one evening, I looked my seventeen-year-old in the eye and said, "We've bumped heads for four years now. It's affecting my marriage, it's disrupting the whole household, and we're not going to live this way anymore. Son, you need to make a decision. Either you come in this house and start living with the kind of attitude and behavior you know is right, whether you believe in God or not, or you need to make other living arrangements. If you can't live in this house with the few nonnegotiable rules we've outlined, then it's time for you to earn a living, figure out where you're going to live, and buy your own food. You'll need to arrange your own transportation and take care of all your bills. We don't want you to do that; it would break my heart and your mother's too. But we're not going to let your attitude and actions ruin every other area of our lives and affect your brothers and sister."

Now that's a drastic measure to take. Don't ever do it lightly, don't ever do it before you've received godly counsel, and don't ever do it as a bluff. It's a last resort, and you need to be prepared to follow through if your child chooses to walk away. My words were strong, but they definitely weren't empty, and my son knew that. He knew my words would be backed up with consequences. I loved him with all my heart and wanted the best for him, but I had exhausted every means available. The next few days were strangely quiet in our home. My son had a big decision to make, and my wife and I were praying and fasting, asking God to move his heart.

When he tells his side of the story, and how he eventually turned back to us and to God, my son doesn't point to how profound my lectures were, or how effective my parenting strategies were. "I saw incredible brokenness," he says. "It wasn't anger. My dad never said, 'What are people going to think?' or 'What will this mean for my job as a pastor?' As I was thinking about why he was so broken, I realized my dad wasn't trying to teach me how to believe or make me into something, he just wanted to share with me the most precious thing he'd ever been given: a relationship with his heavenly Father. That was his life, his breath, his reason for doing everything he did. I began to think, *Maybe there's something there.* So I began to pray, *Lord, if this is real, show me.*"

Faith really is caught more than taught. My words were important, but they would have meant nothing to my teen if they hadn't been backed up by authentic faith. It certainly wasn't perfect faith—our family was always pretty transparent about our failures—but in our home, faith was genuine. And eventually, he realized that all the words were more than just words. After brooding over the issue for a few days, he acknowledged that he knew the right thing to do. It wasn't easy for him, but he chose to adapt his behavior and remain at home.

Pitfalls to Avoid

Words can be powerful in everyday situations as well. Even when your child seems to be ignoring your instructions, your words have the power to build up or to tear down. I know how it feels to let your emotions get the best of you and say something you regret. Every parent has done that at one time or another. I've found the following five parental behaviors to be counterproductive or even destructive. Staying away from these pitfalls keeps your parenting balanced as you verbally discipline your children.

1. *The screaming parent.* A parent who begins to scream is as out of control as the child. As much as possible, you must interact with your child at an adult level of maturity, not a child's. When a parent's voice begins to escalate and your conflict turns into a shouting match, you don't look like the one in charge anymore. Your authority comes from who you are, not from your volume and intensity. Yelling and screaming are counterproductive

   Parents who scream are as out of control as their child. You must interact with your child at an adult level of maturity, not a child's.

   and usually indicate a history of unhealthy communication patterns. After unresolved issues build up, the parent explodes, the child withdraws or rebels, and destructive patterns start to develop in place of discipline.

2. *The all-talk parent.* Kids are pretty shrewd. They're also naturally manipulative. Some parents who tend to be high on the "love" quotient but low on the discipline side of life often find themselves spending long periods of time having "deep talks" about the problem at hand. Smart children will listen attentively and let

you get it out of your system. Their behavior never changes, but you think something happened because you listened to your son or daughter's innermost feelings about why he's disobeying and how hard life is. It's great to talk with your kids about serious issues, but don't make the mistake of thinking that a lot of talk is necessarily going to resolve the big behavioral issues. The long conversation to get to a point of "mutual understanding" is often seen by children as a ritual to play along with until things settle down. You're after behavioral change, not simply an exchange of information or an emotional connection.

3. *The abusive parent.* You may have had a rough past and be left with unresolved anger issues, but losing control and striking a child means you need to go get help. Even being tempted to strike a child out of anger should prompt you to get some counseling.

Keep in mind that verbal abuse can be just as devastating to a child as physical abuse. Words have the power to leave lasting scars. If you have a tendency to berate, humiliate, or insult your child, please follow the same advice I give to physically abusive parents: go get help. No one in professional ministry and counseling is going to think you're a terrible person. They understand how deep the origins of this kind of behavior are, and with God's grace, they'll help you heal.

4. *The closed-lip parent.* When you see the chaos in your household and your spouse keeps telling you that there's a serious problem, I hope you don't simply say, "Kids go through phases like this. He'll grow out of it," and then turn back to your newspaper or TV set. That's called denial. When we are aware of issues that will harm our children and that reflect disobedience to God's standard, we must engage the situation, even if it's uncomfortable.

Some parents are closed-lipped for a different reason—they understand the issue but have adopted a passive "I don't like conflict" attitude and are reluctant to do anything about it. Like a cancer, the problem will grow. If one of your kids is having chronic trouble, ask God for strength and grace, and deal with it.

5. *The lightbulb parent.* Many parents have a tendency to get all fired up about parenting, come up with a plan, have clear expectations, and lay it all out for the family. Then two days later, after the kids have started moving in the right direction, the plans are dropped or the enforcement becomes very irregular. Maybe they required too much energy to monitor, or maybe they go out the window when Mom or Dad has a headache, or maybe a family crisis interrupts the plan. Unfortunately, regardless of the cause, the child experiences a parent who is functioning like a lightbulb. The lightbulb is on, then off, then on again, then off again.

Kids get multiple messages from that kind of inconsistency. If the parent is in a good mood, a clear offense might be ignored. Two days later, the same behavior might get a harsh response. Few things have as much power to discourage children and discredit parents in the eyes of children as inconsistency in discipline. Kids begin to watch their parents closely to see when the lightbulb parent is on and when they can have their way. Usually they know exactly which parent to go to at exactly the right times. That results in misery for the parents, not to mention unclear boundaries for the kids.

Your Game Plan

If the kind of discipline discussed in the last two chapters is new to your family and you need to change some things, you may be wondering where to start. Let me give you a brief game plan that will help you practically apply these principles.

First, identify the top two behavior problems in your home.

Whether they are fights over chores, talking back, disrespect, violating standards, or whatever, they should be fairly obvious. Wherever you and your kids butt heads most often, that's where you want to focus.

Second, honestly evaluate your current parenting pattern. Go back to the four quadrants in chapter 5. Are you too permissive? too strict? Is your love for your child out of balance? Self-evaluation is hard because you're identifying how much of the problem stems from you rather than your child. But you have to address your issues before you can effectively deal with your child's.

Few things have as much power to discourage children and discredit parents in the eyes of children as inconsistency in discipline.

Third, have a family conference. Sit together somewhere comfortable and let your children know you're not mad. Calmly point out the problems in the family system and own up to your part in them. If you haven't been consistent enough, say so. If you feel as if you've been too strict or too lenient, admit it. Tell your children you've asked God to forgive you and then sincerely ask them to forgive you, if and when appropriate.

Once you've done that, you've separated yourself from past practices—and probably begun earning your kids' respect in the process. Now you're ready to lay out your plan by telling them what the misbehavior in question will result in if they keep doing it. You tell them that your desire is to be extremely faithful to God in this matter, and because you love Him and you love your kids, you're going to stick to it. If they're old enough, you can go ahead and work out a contract and let them have a part in creating it.

You can end the conference in a powerful way by joining hands and praying together, asking for God's help to get your household in order. God delights to hear the honest cries of parents and children who realize they need His help and want to be a family that honors

His name. Grace always flows toward humility, and I cannot count the times we sat down as a family, started over by resetting family values and consequences, and saw God bring peace and a new beginning as we trusted Him.

Putting It into Practice

Can you think of an uncomfortable situation you might have been able to avoid in the past month if only you had said no firmly to one of your children?

_____

_____

_____

_____

_____

In addition to being decisive, an important part of discipline is teaching your child to own the consequences of his or her actions. One way to do this is with contracts. When your child clearly understands the consequences that will result from inappropriate behavior, you transfer full responsibility for the outcome to him or her. Identify one way you could use a contract to transfer responsibility to your child.

_____

_____

_____

_____

_____

Keeping in mind the situation you described on page 133, work with your child to complete the chart below. In the first column, describe your child's behavior. In the second column, summarize the disciplinary consequence you and your child have agreed upon as a response to that behavior. (See page 124 for some examples.)

BEHAVIOR:	CONSEQUENCES:

8 / Five Smooth Stones

Once your kids have learned to obey and have begun making decisions out of a desire to please God, what next? Can they really be change-makers in a culture that seems bent in other directions?

One recent event that made parents question their ability to protect their kids from a society that seemed to be spiraling out of control was the 1999 shootings at Columbine High School. Not only were we fearful for our own children; the dynamics of the shootings revealed that our culture and our homes were the petri dish in which this tragedy was cultivated.

The shooters came from upper-middle-class families in a well-to-do suburb in Colorado. Their parents were well educated, and the boys had received professional counseling and anger management classes following an earlier run-in with the law. Yet, their parents seemed taken completely by surprise and shocked to discover the dark side of their sons' lives as revealed on their Web site and personal recordings after the incident.

This school shooting was, in many ways, the tipping point for parents and educators. It was about the sixth such incident within a sixteen-month period, and it surfaced three major fears parents have: (1) Are my children safe at school? (2) Do I really know what's going on inside my child? (3) What can I do to guard my child from the kind of evil influences of our culture that so greatly influenced the Columbine shooters?

As I watched the parents in our church respond to the tragedy and listened to the experts on television, it became clear that the average parent was paralyzed with fear. Blame was spread in many directions, but the end result was a wake-up call to parents, educators, schools, and the media. We had a major problem on our hands that needed to be addressed. Columbine awakened us to the reality that we'd better prepare our children to live in a world that is dangerous to their physical, emotional, and spiritual well-beings.

Unfortunately, most parents were ill-equipped to train their children for battle and resorted to knee-jerk safety measures to insulate their children from society. But the media, the Internet, and the music and movie industry have created a cultural web from which we cannot completely shield our children. Many parents believe it's impossible to raise teenagers who can live winsome and holy lives in the midst of an ever-perverse and evil culture. The result is often an overprotective and dysfunctional approach to parenting. Rather than preparing our children to win life's biggest battles, many attempt to protect their children from those battles.

In the next two chapters, we will challenge some of those assumptions and provide you with the tools to help your children win life's biggest battles. To start the journey, let's look at a young man who shaped his world rather than being shaped by it.

Youth on a Mission

The teenager went down to the front lines of the battle one day to take his brothers some food. They had been fighting a vicious army from the land of their archenemies. The boy entered the military camp only to find that the enemy's most dangerous warrior was taunting this teenager's countrymen and blaspheming the one true God. The enormous hulk of a soldier was vile, spouting all kinds of vulgarities. And no one—not even the teenager's older brothers—had the character and courage to put a stop to it.

Many parents believe it's impossible to raise teenagers who can live winsome and holy lives in the midst of an everperverse and evil culture.

You probably know the story well. The teenager, David, took five smooth stones out of a nearby stream and insisted that the king of Israel let him go out and fight Goliath. A lot was at stake; the duel was like a bet, and if David lost, Israel's armies would have to serve the Philistines. David assured King Saul that he had fought lions and bears and won, with God's help. Saul relented, even though David refused to wear the king's armor, and sent David into battle with just his five stones.

The first stone that David flung from his slingshot hit Goliath in the forehead and ended the battle. But the victory can't be credited to a stone; it was the result of a youth with a lot of character and a passion for God.

David certainly wasn't the only young person used by God to do great things. Daniel was just a teenager when he was taken to Babylon and raised in the king's courts. He was faced with all the privileges of a royal education and service—and all the temptations too. He was a godly boy in a godless kingdom, and he was used powerfully and strategically by the God who was with him to affect a nation's worship.

Joseph was a just a youth when God gave him a radical dream of his future—including a vision of his brothers and parents bowing to him because of his stature. God eventually used Joseph to preserve His chosen people.

Samuel was a very young child when God first began to speak to him. His mother had dedicated him to the service of God, and God accepted her sacrifice with pleasure. Samuel grew in godliness and became an influential priest and judge at a key time in Israel's history. During a rebellious age, Samuel's character was noteworthy. His integrity was crucial during the reign of a self-absorbed and disobedient king.

Centuries later, God fulfilled His plan to save sinful humanity by coming in human flesh. At that time, the chosen people were oppressed by a pagan empire, and pure worship was a rarity even among God's own people. From whose womb was His Son, the Messiah, born? From that of a young teenager who was singled out for her godly character. God's entire salvation plan hinged on a girl with an obedient and worshipful heart.

Those stories should be encouraging. There is a common denominator in each of them: A teenager with a lot of character living in a culture without much at all. The odds were against them. Their parents faced uphill battles every day. Yet God's grace was sufficient to raise great kids in the hardest of times. If you ever feel as if you're living in the hardest of times, remember that. God is in the business of helping small children win epic battles.

Your Kids on the Battlefield

Like David, your children are facing huge battles. The giants they face can be so intimidating that you may be tempted to teach them to cope rather than train them to win. But there's no need to compromise your parenting out of fear. Your children already have

God on their side; there are also five smooth stones you can give them to slay the giants in their lives.

These five stones will help you avoid obsessing about being a perfect parent. I know from experience how easy it is for parents to do that. You wonder if you flicked your wrist hard enough, or if the contracts you made with your kids were too easy on them, or if you leveled a consequence on them that would scar them for life. That's natural. But the key to parenting isn't so much what you do. It's who you are. In this and the next chapter, I want to give you the five smooth stones that you can integrate into your life and the lives of your children. They will find them invaluable on any battlefield and against any giant.

The giants our kids face can be so intimidating that you may be tempted to teach them to cope rather than train them to win.

The First Stone: Teach Them to Suffer Well

Life Myth: Suffering is to be avoided at all costs.

Life Message: Suffering is normal.

Most children growing up in developed countries have gotten the message that suffering is abnormal. When anything goes wrong in their lives, they feel deprived. We've unwittingly created a culture of entitlement. When a crisis comes along, many children want to know who's at fault and why they're getting a raw deal.

Give your children a coherent "theology of suffering." Make sure they grasp the reality of life in a fallen world. They need to know two basic, inalterable facts: (1) Life is hard, but God is good; and (2) Life is unjust, but God is sovereign.

You already know life is hard, but your children may think it's not supposed to be, especially if they believe the messages they get from TV and movies, in which people often don't suffer the consequences of their sin and frequently live charmed lives. You also already know that life is unfair, but your children probably really struggle with that idea. Most don't understand how someone who doesn't study for a test can still get an A, or why the coach's son gets to play when they're the ones who have been practicing hard for years. They will come to you sometimes and cry about how unfair something is, and as much as you want to, you won't be able to change their situation. You need to prepare them for a life of difficulties and disappointments. You don't want your words to depress them, but you also don't serve them well by teaching that life will always treat them well. They need to know whom to turn to—first to you, and then as they mature, to God—when life lets them down.

> *Most children growing up in developed countries have gotten the message that suffering is abnormal.*

One way to begin teaching them this principle is by telling them the story of Joseph very early in their lives. You can find it in Genesis 37–50, and if it becomes a regular bedtime story, your children will know what it means to trust God when they think they've gotten a raw deal.

You remember Joseph, I'm sure. He was the teenager who had the dream about his parents and siblings bowing down to him. His eleven brothers knew that he was his father's favorite, and they resented him for it. So they sold him to traders who carted him off to Egypt as a slave. Joseph could have griped about wasting his life as a servant—or later as a dungeon prisoner—because he spent years in a seemingly futile situation. But Joseph trusted God, and God proved to be both sovereign and good. God eventually raised Joseph to a position of great power and used him to save his family from a famine.

After Joseph's most painful and difficult trials were over, he was able to make a landmark statement about God's sovereignty. He told the brothers who had betrayed him: "You intended to harm me, but God intended it for good" (Genesis 50:20). Years in slavery and prison had not stolen his faith in God. As far as we know, he didn't bitterly complain about his situation, and he didn't feel entitled to compensation for it. He accepted his brothers' treachery as part of God's course for his life, and he was grateful for the blessings that finally resulted.

Your ultimate goal in the area of suffering is for your children to follow the example of Jesus. That's where Peter pointed Christians in the early church when they were under the heavy hand of persecution. "Christ suffered for you, leaving you an example, that you should follow in his steps. 'He committed no sin, and no deceit was found in his mouth.' When they hurled their insults at him, he did not retaliate; when he suffered, he made no threats" (1 Peter 2:21-23). You can teach your children to respond to suffering as Jesus did—to entrust themselves to the sovereign God who judges justly—rather than to be consumed by bitterness like so many other people in the world.

God will take the unfair, unjust, painful, evil circumstances of your children's lives and mix them with His goodness and sovereignty. Your children need to know that they will suffer—Jesus even guaranteed it (John 16:33)—but that God is good and He is ultimately in control. Whatever injustice they face, God will vindicate them eventually. Whatever hardship they go through, God can bring fruitfulness and blessing out of it. They can face anything in life if you've taught them those principles from an early age.

That will set them apart from the rest of the world. Do you realize how many people are eaten up with bitterness, or how many people have anger fantasies about an ex-spouse who cheated on them or an ex-business partner who deceived them? The world is full of people whose souls are poisoned with resentment and grief from all the times they've been knocked around. They get ulcers, suffer from depression, and emotionally withdraw from others because they can't handle any more pain. They grow disillusioned and live without a sense of purpose. You don't want your children to live like that.

LIVING OUT THE LESSON: TURN SUFFERING INTO OPPORTUNITY

How can you help them grow through suffering rather than be beaten down by it? Take three steps. *First, ask them about their concerns and give them the freedom to answer honestly.* Because we live in a culture that has essentially become a happiness cult, we want to fix all our children's problems. And usually we don't just want to fix them, we want to fix them *quickly.* When something seems wrong with your children, ask them what the problem is. Don't let them get by with "nothing" as an answer. Keep probing until you uncover the problem and can help them deal with it.

Once they've shared their troubles, empathize with them. Identify with their pain and get into their world. Let them know you really want to listen and hear what's on their hearts. Say things like, "Oh, I know that hurts. I feel for you. That's really a tough situation." Don't get into the fix-it mode—"That's not right!"; "I'll call your teacher"; "Let me talk to your coach"—at least not immediately. They're going to hurt sometimes, and your job is to teach them to hurt in a way that's redemptive. Pray with them. Give God a chance. You aren't always going to be there with them. God will. Invite Him into your children's situations so they'll learn how to do that.

The second step is to find out where they're suffering. You've already gotten them to tell you what they're concerned about. Now seek to move beyond the troubling circumstances and dig down to the root issues. How is their heart really hurting? What kind of questions are they asking? Are they wrestling with doubts? feeling betrayed?

nurturing resentment? Every human being has some deep wounds. Here it is important to listen not only with your ears, but with your heart. What are they *not* saying? What beliefs and emotions are they processing? You want to be aware of your children's wounds so you can help them deal with them in a healthy, redemptive way.

Remember, the first stone in your child's pouch is to learn that suffering is normal. It will either make them or break them, depending on how they process it and respond to it. Once they know you care and really understand what they are going through, it's time to provide some perspective and use this difficulty as a teachable moment.

Your kids are going to hurt sometimes, and your job is to teach them to hurt in a way that's redemptive.

The third step is to align their suffering with Scripture and begin shaping your children's worldview through biblical lenses. Bring the Word of God alongside their pain and reaffirm who God is, how much He cares for His children, and how He works all things together for the good of those who love Him. Pain has a way of distorting our perceptions of God and others. Scripture has a way of bringing the right perspective back into focus. Open the Bible with gentleness and take them not only to God's Word, but to a God who really knows and feels our pain. Avoid making Scripture an "answer book" of clichés. Open it as a source of help and healing from your heavenly Father, who wants to comfort you and your child. Don't let your children experience the pain without the corrective lenses of Scripture.

One of the most talented musicians ever to come out of our church in Santa Cruz was a young man named John. He had a musical gift from God that amazed me. He watched someone play the piano, and without a lesson he was playing the piano almost as well a short time later. He saw someone play a mandolin and thought it looked cool, so he picked it up and could play it almost immediately. He played the guitar, had a fantastic voice, and wrote music. He was an immensely creative and talented guy.

John hung out at our house frequently and played music with my sons in our garage. I was always amazed at how skinny John was because he put away so much food when he spent time at our house. John and my son Jason would have jam sessions and write music together. They went away to different colleges, but they always got back together when they could to play their music, and they got better and better at it.

I still remember the day we found out that the reason John was so skinny was that he had cancer. I drove to the hospital, sat with his parents, and read Psalm 46 to them. We spent a lot of hours and days there together. John understood that he was going to die, and over several months he grew as emaciated as someone in a concentration camp. His buddies stood around his bed and sang and prayed with him, watching him physically waste away. It was an incredibly painful experience.

Jason and I went to his home the day before John died. We talked and prayed with him, and Jason got to spend one last afternoon with his best friend. Leaving John's home and knowing he had only hours to live, Jason and I sat in the car for a while and talked. I'll always remember what he said: "Dad, I don't get it. John is only twenty-five years old. He's got more talent in his little finger than I've got in my whole body. I work and work at this stuff, and John just does it naturally. Why would God do this?"

What does a dad say? How do you help your son learn to suffer well in a situation like that? How do you help him process the fact that suffering is normal? How do you avoid cliché answers and yet align life's tragedies with the truth of Scripture? As in almost any situation, what we model communicates more than anything we say. My son had seen my broken heart and tears as we gathered around John's bed for the last time.

In my brokenness, I said, "Son, I don't understand everything, but I know God is good. I know God loves John and He's sovereign. We live in a fallen world, and sometimes bad things happen to good people, and God allows it. Sometimes God fulfills His purposes in a person in eighty-five years, and sometimes He accomplishes them in only twenty-five." And we talked about how hard this was to swallow and what a mystery God's purposes can be sometimes. We brought this situation in line with Scripture, remembering the story of Joseph and the example of Jesus, who entrusted His life to a faithful Father. And then we just cried.

The Second Stone: Teach Them to Work "unto the Lord"

Life Myth: Work is to be endured as a means to a higher standard of living.

Life Message: You were created to work.

Not only do you want to arm your children with a theology of suffering, you also want to instill in them a "theology of work." The life message they need is that they were created to work.

First, your children need to know that work is a calling, not a job. The word *vocation* comes from the Latin verb for "to call" or "to summon." It's the same root from which we get "voice," "vocal," and "evoke." The implication is that work is a personal dynamic, not an impersonal status. Your children must understand that what they do in life (vocation) should flow out of their relationship with God. It's more than a choice; it's a response to how God has formed and equipped them.

Most kids don't know that because we live in a culture that emphasizes employment in terms of "upward mobility." Parents often knowingly or unknowingly push their children to get into the best schools and get the best training so they can get the best job that will provide them with the best salary for their future. It becomes a matter of material success. Other parents stress to their children that they can do whatever they dream of in life. It's the natural conclusion of a society that has bought into the "happiness cult" philosophy. When a child asks his mom or dad what he should major in, those parents respond, "Oh, honey, it doesn't matter to me. Whatever makes you happy." Neither of these emphases is biblical.

God has a specific purpose for your children's life, just as He did with David (Psalm 139:16), with Jeremiah (Jeremiah 1:5), and the rest of us (Ephesians 2:10). He designed them with individual DNA, both physically and, in a sense, spiritually. He has a calling on all of your children, and you need to help them discover not simply what they can do to make money, not simply what they can do to make themselves happy, but how God wants them to serve Him. That's a discovery process that takes time, but God will guide anyone who asks Him to. You need to lead your kids to pray for direction from God and ask such hard questions as, "How do you think God has designed you to fit into His Kingdom?" and "What spiritual gifts has He given you?"

Does that mean God isn't interested in your children making money or being happy? Of course not. He wants the best for them. But only He knows what the absolute best is. Only He knows exactly what He designed them to do.

That idea may go against the grain of our culture, but consider this: About 75 percent of Americans don't like their jobs. They feel as if they're stuck in a rut, and most of them live from weekend to weekend and vacation to vacation, only tolerating their jobs until they get the next break from them.

Don't get the impression here that I'm talking about everyone being called into a professional ministry position. God has designed some people to be doctors, some to be plumbers, some to be lawyers, some to be carpenters, some to do landscape design, some to go into business for themselves, some to stay at home with children, and so on. Christians are to fill the world as musicians, artists, scientists, linguists, teachers, laborers, computer experts, social workers, and anything else that might fit into the Kingdom of God. Your job as a parent is to help each of your children discover his or her unique calling.

Second, your children need to know that work is sacred. When God put Adam and Eve in the Garden, He gave them work to do. They were to tend the Garden and subdue the earth. That was *before* the Fall, not after. Anyone who believes that *work* is a dirty word, as much of our society does, doesn't understand how God made us. Work isn't a result of the Fall. Maybe the extreme difficulty and periodic futility of work is a result of sin, but the need for it isn't. It is ordained by God, and we were designed for it.

Teach your kids that work is a sacred stewardship, not an evil to put up with. This is an attitude they need to pick up from you. And remember that how you act shapes them more than what you say. Even if you are part of the majority of people who don't like their jobs, be careful what you say in front of your children. If you come home from work every day and talk about how you can't stand your job and can't wait until your next day off, you're sending your kids a clear message that work is a pain in the neck. If you're complaining about how difficult it is staying at home with the kids all day, you're preaching to them about how meaningless you think your job is. Certainly, you don't want to go to the other extreme and pretend that your work is always fun and rewarding. I also don't mean that you should never mention that you're tired or say that you need a break from your work; they need to learn about the value of rest too. Just make sure that you speak of your vocation with respect, as something God has entrusted you with.

Third, your children need to know that work flows from God's design and purpose for their lives. There's a reason that some kids are athletic and others are artistic, that some are good in English and others are good in math. And that principle applies to personality too. Some kids are quiet and withdrawn by design, and others were meant to enjoy being in front of a crowd. These traits are neutral, neither good nor bad.

What's bad is when parents try to force an introverted kid to be an extrovert, as though something is wrong with him; or when they try to subdue an extrovert because his outgoing nature comes across as "acting out" rather than an asset. A parent who pushes a shy child into a career in sales or politics isn't sensitive to how God made that child, just as a parent who tries to steer a gregarious kid to a job in a research library or an office cubicle isn't sensitive to God's design either. You want your introverts to learn social skills and your extroverts to learn appropriate behavior, but you don't want to change their personalities. There's a purpose in their personalities and talents, and they need to embrace their attributes, not reform them. Focus on building their strengths rather than becoming preoccupied with their apparent weaknesses.

Study the characteristics God has given to your children. Then help your children cultivate those distinctives and refine them for future fruitfulness. Help them look for opportunities to be who they are and fulfill their calling. Pushing them to act contrary to the way God designed them is like giving them a death sentence. You may have dreams for your children, but once you recognize how God made them, you may not want those dreams fulfilled. You will guarantee frustration for your children if you try to fit square pegs into round holes. Our job is to cooperate with God's agenda—not fulfill our agenda vicariously through our kids, train them for a lucrative career, or teach them to climb the social ladder. We want them to find joy by becoming the piece of the puzzle that fits into God's kingdom just the way He intended.

In Scripture, God repeatedly affirmed people like Joseph, David, Daniel, Jeremiah, Stephen, and anyone else who had the kind of faith that led to humble obedience—even when their positions or visible accomplishments were hard to see. When your child finds how she was made to fit into God's world, the result can be powerful: deep, internal joy and lasting, high-impact fruit. That makes your child a vocational success, by God's definition. It also makes you a parenting success.

Focus on building your children's strengths rather than becoming preoccupied with their apparent weaknesses.

Fourth, your children need to know how to work for an audience of One. Teach them to work not to make an impression on people, but to serve as an offering to the Lord.

I remember when my mom used to make me vacuum. She actually wanted me to move the coffee table so I could vacuum under it thoroughly. She also wanted me to vacuum under the rug. I'd think to myself, *No one can see those things under the coffee table, and they certainly can't see under the rug.* Same thing when I had to clean up my room. I'd jam all my clothes into the drawers, and the room would look great.

The problem was that my mom would come in and inspect. She would open the drawers and look under the coffee table and say, "No, that's not what I meant. Try again." I was doing my work for the outward impression it would make, not for the eyes that see everything.

Like a kid trying to get by on shortcuts, many of us develop an attitude about work that says, "It only matters if it's visible." We avoid being thorough, as if God isn't watching. But the Lord sees everything. If your children consider themselves successful simply because they impress other people, they will run the risk of pleasing the world without pleasing God. They need to learn that everything they do is for the glory of God. Their homework is for Him, not for their teacher. They cut the lawn for Him, not for you. They clean up their room for His eyes, not yours. Help them memorize Colossians 3:23-24: "Whatever you do, work at it with all your heart, as working for the Lord, not for men, since you know that you will receive an inheritance from the Lord as a reward. It is the Lord Christ you are serving." I'm sure my children got sick of quoting Colossians 3:23-24 in our home as they learned to redo a job that was not done well or "as unto the Lord." But years later, now that they're grown, all four of them have an excellent work ethic—and, more importantly, an understanding of whom they're working for. If your children learn that, they can go through life with a satisfaction in work that doesn't depend on who else is watching.

Although teaching Colossians 3:23-24 is important, modeling it is the real key to transmitting it into your children's value system. If you constantly complain about changing diapers, getting up in the morning, doing yard work, spending an occasional extra hour or two at the office, or completing any other task that's part of your vocation or home responsibilities, what attitude do you think your children will pick up? But as you model doing everything as a gift to Jesus Christ—because you work ultimately for Him, not for people—your children will intuitively learn to do likewise. That makes even cleaning the bathroom or paying the bills sacred acts of service.

Do you realize how much this attitude will benefit both you and your children? Anyone who works "unto the Lord" will have a leg up on everyone who only does what is necessary and sufficient. The world is full of people just trying to get by. When you and your kids serve the Lord in your work, you not only become valued employees in the eyes of the world now, you will receive the Lord's inheritance later. No employer can match those benefits.

LIVING OUT THE LESSON: HELP YOUR CHILDREN DISCOVER THEIR CALLING

How can you help your children learn to work "unto the Lord"?

1. *Give them weekly jobs and expect them to be done with a good attitude.* Every child needs to have regular chores that you inspect. Teach them that doing them with slumped shoulders and rolling eyes is not acceptable. You can show them how and work alongside them, but they need to have multiple opportunities for hands-on work. What specific chores have you assigned your children? Start them early. Make them fun. Increase the level of responsibility as they get older. Give them tasks that will stretch them. When they've mastered one task, give them another one to learn. Use charts with their chores on it, so they can feel good about how much they've accomplished. Offer them rewards for faithful obedience, just as God does for us. Whatever it takes, encourage them to fulfill their responsibilities with a willing heart that can celebrate their successes.

2. *Study their gifts.* If I sat down with you, took out a notepad, and started asking you questions about your child, would you be able to give me detailed answers? Who are her three closest friends? What does she get most excited about? What is she really good at that she enjoys doing? What does she daydream about? What are her fears? If you can't answer those questions, you don't know your child well enough to help her discover her calling. You need to understand the personality and passions of your child well enough to guide her into the vocation God has designed her for.

   My son Eric was so shy when he was a little boy that it was painful to watch. He had absolutely no confidence. When he was about seven, I put skates on him one morning and told him we couldn't go back inside until noon. He was so afraid of failure that he didn't want to try to learn to skate. It was the same when he learned to ride a bike. I told him we were going to stay outside until he learned. Sounds harsh, doesn't it? But he wouldn't know how to skate or ride a bike today if we hadn't approached it that way. I knew he had to be pushed to break through his fears because I had taken the time to understand his personality.

When it was time for him to go away to college, he had a hard time making a decision. He was leaning toward spending another year at the local community college by default. I've got nothing against community colleges, but I knew the personality of my son well enough to know that this one wasn't for him. Santa Cruz is very laid back, and many local students had been in college for ten or twelve years. We'd go to restaurants and see MBAs waiting tables simply to earn enough money to sustain a life of surfing. One of my sons went there for two years and was so focused it was easy for him to move on. Eric was different. He could easily have ended up as one of those kids with twenty semesters' worth of parking stickers on his back bumper.

I told Eric he couldn't attend the local college. I'd allow him to do a nationwide search for the right school, and I'd even fly with him to his top three choices. But making the easy decision by default was not going to be an option for him. He ended up going out of state, falling in love with biology, continuing his education beyond undergraduate school, and becoming a physical therapist. Why? Because Theresa and I had studied him for eighteen years and knew what it would take to help him find his calling. It would have been easy to let his education unfold in the easiest way for him, but that wouldn't have been fulfilling for him in the long run. It wouldn't have prepared him to fit into God's plan.

When your children come to you, they're a little bundle of gifts and opportunities. They are designed to fulfill a specific purpose that was prepared just for them. You are to nurture the characteristics God has put within them and help protect them from missing their purposes. Even if they stumble along the way and pursue directions God never intended for them—you can find plenty of examples of this, like Paul's legalistic Pharisaism, for one—help them understand how He uses all of their backgrounds to accomplish His purposes. Nothing is wasted, not even mistakes. Bring them back to the feet of the Father who made them. Give them a very clear message that they are *not* what they do; they are to *do what they are*. They are defined by who God made them to be, and what they do must flow out of that.

The Third Stone: Teach Them to Manage Their Wealth Wisely

Life Myth: Everything you have in life is yours to use as you see fit.

Life Message: Your life is a sacred stewardship.

God owns everything. The culture your child is growing up in doesn't act as if that's true. Even among Christians, the prevalent perspective is that we are to give God 10 percent and do whatever we want with the remaining 90 percent. But according to the Bible, we own nothing. God entrusts us with a wealth of resources (which include time, talent, treasure, opportunities—the whole package of who we are and what we have) to manage as wise stewards.

Teach your kids early what Paul told the Corinthians when he asked this question: "What do you have that you did not receive?" (1 Corinthians 4:7). The answer, of course, is "nothing." You want your children to have the mind-set that nothing belongs to them. It's all God's, and they only manage certain resources for a season.

Teach them also that God expects a positive return on His investment. He's the ultimate investment banker. He has given each of your children brains, talents, interests, a personality, the material resources of your family, and time. They will be accountable to Him for what they do with those resources. Their portfolios will be evaluated, and greater rewards come to those who have been wise stewards.

The point of that truth is not to put pressure on you or your children. God doesn't cross His arms, frown at us, and tell us we'd better produce results or else. His ultimate purpose is that we share in His joy. The better we manage God's resources, the more joy He will share with us. We can see that early in Scripture, in Genesis 1:26, where God creates human beings in His own image and gives them a role as co-creators and co-laborers in the world. It's the first command in Scripture: God tells humanity to manage what He owns. We are designed to be His partners, working with Him to produce beautiful and wonderful results. We can demonstrate His glory and spread the message of His mercy, reaping eternal fruit in the process. This is an opportunity, not a demand.

This principle is also clear in the Gospels. The point of the parable of the talents in Matthew 25:14-30 is that those who have been faithful with whatever God has given them will be entrusted with more. They will have greater blessing and more joy. The master in the parable doesn't judge his servants by how much they have to work with. He judges them by what they do with what they have been given. Your children must grow up with an understanding that the things they have are really God's, and they have an amazing opportunity to partner with Him to multiply those resources.

At the end of their stewardship is a tremendous reward if they have been faithful.

Your kids won't get that message from society. Their peers will speak the language of "my things, my time, my money, my skills." They will have friends who feel entitled, who complain that the expensive Christmas presents they received weren't the right style or size or model, or who act as if they deserve more than what they already have. Your children will have to swim against the stream a little if they are to learn to live as managers of God's resources. The idea of stewardship is not a natural concept among fallen human beings, so it has to be clearly and intentionally taught.

Sadly, your children may not pick up the principle of Christian stewardship at church either. Even many churchgoers believe that they own their stuff, their time, and their abilities and speak in terms of "my house, my car, my 401(k), my time . . ." Few Christians realize, at least to the point of practicing their belief, that these things were given to them "on loan" from God. According to some research, the average believer gives roughly 2.6 percent of his or her income to the Lord's work, and that lack of priority is being passed down to the next generation.[9] Your children must see the commitment to giving in you, or they won't see it at all. They need to hear and see you treat all that you have as a sacred stewardship from God. This concept of stewardship and gratitude will be caught as you give generously and cheerfully of your time, talent, and treasure to help others and honor God.

Your children need to know that your heart is where your treasure is. The point of giving is to free your heart from the master of greed. Don't give your children the impression that God needs their money. The degree of a person's stewardship is an indication

> *Stewardship is not a natural concept among fallen human beings, so it has to be clearly and intentionally taught.*

of what his or her heart really worships. If kids get the message that it's normal for people to always be asking "what's in it for me," they will never know how to worship God. They will also miss out on the blessing of the parable of the talents: "Enter into the joy of your master" (Matthew 25:21, NASB).

LIVING OUT THE LESSON: PRACTICAL WAYS TO TEACH THAT GOD OWNS IT ALL

Practically, how can you help your children learn that they are stewards, not owners? First, teach them the principle of Luke 16:10 (NASB): "He who is faithful in a very little thing is faithful also in much; and he who is unrighteous in a very little thing is unrighteous also in much." When my kids were small, they each had three jars to put money in: one for giving, one for saving, and one for spending. It was a very simple procedure; every time they got money, one dime would go into the giving jar, one into the saving jar, and eight into the spending jar. When they were young, their allowance would be in dimes to make it easier for them. By the time they were older, they had learned proportional giving, but the 10-10-80 formula was a great place to start. As they grew older, we would provide them the opportunity to give over and above their tithes by adopting as a family various causes—an orphanage in Russia one year, support for a child through a ministry like World Vision or Compassion International, etc. These additional gifts were never compulsory, but as they saw the needs of the world, they learned to give from their hearts. They developed a pattern of giving, saving, and spending that has continued into their adulthood.

Those are the three purposes for money, and kids are never too young to learn them. Every time mine dropped a dime in that giving jar, it would remind them that God owns all there is and is worthy of the first portion of all we receive. Every time they dropped a dime in the saving jar, they were reminded that money is to be used with planning and purpose and that delayed gratification is an important part of life. And every time they dropped eight dimes in the spending jar, they were reminded of the generosity of God and the privilege of being a steward. They would still have to spend that portion wisely, using some of it to help other people and weighing personal spending decisions carefully. But it helped them get in the habit of being God-centered and others-centered in their finances.

That's not that hard to do. It will take some planning and effort, but it isn't complicated. You can then transfer the concepts they've learned with money to other areas of life, like time and talents. Give them a weekly planner when they get into junior high so they can begin to manage their time well. Help them think of ways to use their talents for the benefit of your family and your church. Your children will learn to think through issues and live intentional lives, maximizing the return on God's investment in them. And the end result will be deep, lasting joy.

The battles your children face are real, and these three stones—as well as the two in the next chapter—are crucial core values and practices without which they cannot win the war. But in the every-day pressures of raising children in a fallen world, let me encourage you to look for opportunities to instill these first three life messages into the heart and mind of your child. These "smooth stones" can slay the giants they face daily—and those they will face in the years to come.

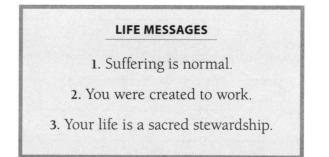

LIFE MESSAGES

1. Suffering is normal.

2. You were created to work.

3. Your life is a sacred stewardship.

Putting It into Practice

Become a student of your child by asking a few probing questions to get to know his or her heart.

Ask your child, "What are you most concerned about?" Record and reflect on his or her answers below.

_____

_____

_____

_____

Ask him or her, "What makes you feel afraid?"

_____

_____

_____

_____

Now consider some signs that may help point to your child's vocational calling in life.

My child's favorite things:

_____

_____

_____

My child's dreams:

_____

_____

_____

My child's gifts and talents:

_____

_____

_____

9 / When All Else Fails

When my children were very young and I was very inexperienced, I tended to focus on the specifics of parenting. Like many of you, I was concerned about everything: what they ate, how much of it they ate, and whether it was good for them. I was consumed with individual homework assignments, sports teams, social skills development, biblical teaching, and getting along with one another. And as we've discussed, all of these are important and have their place.

As we come to the conclusion of our time together on these pages, and as I look back on the lives of my four children who have a passion for Christ, I realize that there are two big-picture issues that we parents must keep before us. We must remember that our children will face two recurring situations until the day they die: (1) Making decisions about what is right and what is wrong; and (2) Learning to recover from the decisions that are wrong. Like us, our children need to learn to make wise choices, and they need to learn that failure is never final. In this chapter, we'll explore the final two "smooth stones" that will help them do that.

The Fourth Stone: Teach Them to Make Wise Decisions

Life Myth: Only you can decide the best, most fulfilling way to live your life.

Life Message: Holy living allows you to experience God's best for your life.

Wisdom is learning to live according to God's design. Scripture promises that as we make wise decisions that reflect God's character and the instructions of His Word, we will be blessed. But often the way we learn to make wise decisions is by making unwise decisions and dealing with the consequences. Your children will face myriad choices in their lifetimes, and the older they get, the more decisions they'll make apart from your presence. The key then is to help them make wise decisions and to learn that grace is available from you and from God when they fail.

> *Our children need to learn to make wise choices, and they need to learn that failure is never final.*

Our children's decision-making abilities will either make or break their lives. No pressure, right? But this isn't about perfection, it's about consistency. They will make some bad decisions, to be sure, but they really need the tools to establish decision patterns so that more often than not they're moving in the right direction. Encouraging wise decision making begins when you teach them a "theology of holiness."

God is holy. We sometimes think that He is similar to a human being, just magnified millions of times. He's not—He's completely, totally "other." He's more awesome, more pure, more compassionate, and more loving than we can possibly imagine. He is in a different category from anything else, and our children will never become holy themselves—and make wise decisions—until they understand that.

God is absolute truth. He doesn't define truth, He *is* truth. Whatever flows out of His being is absolute and unchanging. That means that we live with an understanding that some things are right and some things are wrong. We don't get to choose which verses of the Bible to obey, because it's all inspired by the One who is true. His laws and standards are given for our protection. As much as our culture will try to convince our kids that truth is relative, we have to teach them that it isn't.

What does this mean? Your children are designed to be holy—set apart for God's special use. They were made in His image to be filled with His Spirit in order to commune with Him and to fulfill their individual callings in His power. We discussed earlier how the word *holiness* has gotten a bad rap; in its biblical usage, it's winsome and joyful, and it's a privilege.

Your children may be afraid of what it means to live a "holy" lifestyle. Assure them that you aren't going to send them off to a stone building where they have to wear long black robes and carry massive Bibles, or that they won't have to go through life with a "praise the Lord" sticker on their bumper and a narrow view of everyone around them. Holiness as God defines it is a privilege and a joy. Instill in them a sense of excitement about God's special purposes for them.

Your children may be afraid of what it means to live a "holy" lifestyle.

But also make it very clear that those special purposes come with some high standards for their own good. There are boundaries that can't be crossed: always tell the truth, walk in integrity, no sex outside of marriage, be a good steward—all our actions should fit with the character of God. Let them know that just as gravity would be their adversary if they were to jump off a building, so God's righteousness will be their adversary if they choose to ignore it. God's laws are like guardrails that will keep them from destruction. The positive side of His laws is that they are accompanied with outrageous blessings that most people never know. The greatest possible joy and fulfillment in life come from honoring God through holiness.

If your children understand holiness correctly, they will learn to make good decisions not simply out of fear, but out of a positive response to Christ. Their decisions will flow out of a desire to be Christlike—to partner with God and to share His joy.

LIVING OUT THE LESSON: HELP YOUR CHILD DISCERN BETWEEN GOOD AND EVIL

Practically, here are some ways to help your children understand God's holiness, which is a prerequisite for understanding their role in life. When they're young, read them stories that will impress the holiness of God into their hearts and minds. For example, in Exodus 3, Moses was told to take his shoes off as he stood at the burning bush. Why? Because he was on holy ground. Isaiah heard the angels saying, "Holy, holy, holy, is the Lord Almighty," which in Hebrew is akin to saying God is "holiest." (English adjectives follow the pattern of "holy, holier, and holiest," while Hebrew adjectives are repeated to indicate degree and intensity.) Fiction is more subtle but very effective in impacting a child's mind. In *The Chronicles of Narnia*, which our family read even at ages our kids would be embarrassed to admit, Aslan (the Christ figure) is often spoken of

> *If your children under-stand holiness correctly, they will learn to make good decisions not simply out of fear, but out of a positive response to Christ.*

in hushed whispers and with awe. These and thousands of other stories resonate with clear distinctions between good and evil.

The flip side of filling your children with an understanding of holiness is screening unholy things from them. The amount of garbage our kids are exposed to through TV, movies, and video games is incredible, and it can have disastrous results. You don't have to look too far to find examples of those results—the influence of violent video games on the Columbine killers has been widely reported, as have numerous other links between crime and that segment of the culture. As a society, our tolerance level of murders and immorality in the entertainment media is alarming. Imagine serving your children a healthy, well-rounded meal for supper—a plate full of tasty portions of meat, vegetables, and whole grains—and then topping it off with a dash of arsenic. "Just a little won't hurt" is a bad philosophy for both dieting and spiritual growth. The saying about computers is true: "Garbage in, garbage out." If you don't want garbage coming out of your kids, don't let garbage in.

The average child in America is in front of the television or computer screen as much as three or four hours a day—nearly thirty hours per week—according to many surveys, and that's not how life was meant to be lived.[10] If that's the steady diet your children are consuming, there's no way they will grow up with sharp discernment of good and evil or with the ability to make consistently wise decisions.

If you don't want garbage coming out of your kids, don't let garbage in.

That may sound like a huge generalization, but consider this: The physical law of "you are what you eat" also works spiritually. You are what you think. God's Word teaches us that as a person thinks in his heart, so he is (Proverbs 23:7, NKJV). It also says, "Above all else, guard your heart, for it is the wellspring of life"

(Proverbs 4:23). According to the Bible, what goes on inside your children's mind is a matter of great concern. As your child develops and grows, an hour of church on Sunday and a few minutes of family devotions here and there cannot compete with twenty-plus hours of indiscriminate entertainment each week. So open your home to the media very, very cautiously. If your child is a product of his thoughts, the most important decision you can make is what goes into that precious mind of your child.

In order to get your family back in balance, you may want to try a media fast for a couple of weeks: no TV, no video games, no movies, no radio, nothing. (When your children are small, you have total control of their viewing habits, so two weeks should be easy to implement. But if that seems impossible for older kids, start small, perhaps with three days, and then do it periodically and increase the length of the fast.) Your kids (and probably you too) will go nuts the first few days, but it will cleanse your minds of a lot of the spiritual toxins you've put into them. A couple of weeks later, you may be surprised at what you find. Commercials that didn't faze you before are now appalling. Language and explicit scenes from shows you used to watch will seem pretty shocking. You'll begin to realize how subtly and seriously your family was sucked into a culture that can't discern between right and wrong. It's a good way to recalibrate your soul—and that of your family— from time to time.

I'm not saying, of course, that your family should never watch TV or go to a movie. This isn't a legalistic formula for keeping your kids pure. While you certainly don't want to use MTV for a babysitter or encourage your kids to learn to play video games better than they can relate to other people, there's nothing wrong with a little whole- some entertainment. Our family, for example, chose not to turn the TV on during school nights, but on Friday nights we would often pop some popcorn and watch a good movie. I think it's important for children to know that TV can be used positively, and making it completely off-limits overestimates its power.

As a family, you can decide what standards you need to have. Communicate those standards clearly to your children so they know what kinds of movies are off-limits and can make on-the-spot decisions when spending the night with someone or going out with a group of friends. (Our daughter, Annie, in particular, was able to graciously but firmly back out of group activities when they violated her convictions, and we were always happy to go pick her up and bring her home.) Our family spent some time outlining our reasons for our standards: Romans 8:5-8, Romans 12:2, and Colossians 3:1-4 all speak of how a Christian is to fill his or her mind with truth, not with sinful things. Understanding these passages helped our children realize that we weren't being legalistic, but were motivated by a desire to fellowship with God and serve Him wholeheartedly. When we balance out our rules and restrictions with fun and appropriate entertainment, our kids see that our standards are not designed to make them miserable, but to help them enjoy life God's way.

Even when your standards are right on target for your family, the reality is that sometimes your children will fail to live up to them—just like all of us failed to live up to the standards our parents gave us. The fifth stone is one of the most important principles you can teach your kids to help them live in the grace of God, even when they fail.

Fifth Stone: When All Else Fails, Teach Them to Live Grace-Filled Lives

Life Myth: Failure is final.

Life Message: You were created to receive grace and to give grace.

I hope that in the pages of this book, you've picked up my desire to be honest about how often I've failed. If not, let me emphasize it here: I've failed a lot. My wife has failed a lot, my kids have failed a lot, and I'm going to go out on a limb and guess that you've probably failed a lot too. And you know what? Next week we're all probably going to fail again. And it won't be the last time.

Authentic living in the light of God's glory is not about being perfect but about living grace-filled lives in which we make progress in our relationships with Jesus and with each other. In the midst of a fallen world, our intimacy can grow, our love can develop, our purity can increase, and we can win many of our battles. But that progress sometimes comes in fits and starts, and sometimes it takes a step or two backward. When your kids fail, how will they respond? You have to give them a "theology of grace."

First, you have to teach your children what grace is. It is the unmerited, unconditional love of God toward us. It's the complete opposite of a performance-based love that says, "I love you if . . ." or "I love you because . . ." God doesn't love us "if" or "because"—ever. He will never love any one of us any more than He does right at this moment. There's nothing we can do, positively or negatively, to change His love.

> **Authentic living in the light of God's glory is not about being perfect but about living grace-filled lives.**

Does that mean there are no consequences for sin? Of course not. God doesn't buy into the "tolerance" definition of love. We will have serious struggles if we don't follow His Word. But He disciplines us for disobedience not because He's mad, but because He loves us. Everything He does in our lives and circumstances runs through the filter of divine, unconditional love. He's eager to be our friend (John 15:15), He collects our tears in a bottle (Psalm 56:8, NASB), He rejoices over us with singing (Zephaniah 3:17), and He understands (Psalm 139:1-5; Hebrews 4:15). Your kids need to know that, and they need to catch it from you.

They will have a hard time believing this truth. Why? Because very little else in their life operates this way. School is performance-based. Sports are performance-based. Music is performance-based. Even a lot of what they do in church and in their devotions—how often they read their Bible, how much time they spend praying, how many good deeds they've done—is performance-based. They'll get in performance mode in almost every area of their life. If they are ever going to understand grace, they'll have to learn it from the Word of God. And if they are ever going to see a picture of it, they'll probably have to see it in the way you relate to them and others.

Grace is free. It can't be earned. It's extremely costly—it cost God the life of His Son, so it isn't cheap. But it's free. And though your children will grow up in performance systems and one day apply for a performance-based job, the culture of your home needs to be completely different. When they fail, your kids need to see and experience unconditional love. They need to have the freedom to fall down and an open invitation to get back up.

A lot of children—adults too, for that matter—get the impression that if they read their Bible every day, have a regular prayer time, attend church regularly, tithe 10 percent of their income, and contribute to clothing and canned food drives, everything will go well for them. God will see their obedience and reward them for it. He will, of course, but often not like they think. And when they don't see the correlation they expect, they start to wonder. Maybe they got that flat tire because they cut their quiet time short that day. Perhaps that argument with their

> *When they fail, your kids need to see and experience unconditional love. They need to have the freedom to fall down and an open invitation to get back up.*

spouse was discipline for missing church on Sunday. Maybe they slipped up somewhere and broke their bargain with God. That's a stressful, dismal way to live.

Does our disobedience affect our relationship with God? Does our intimacy with the Lord and with others suffer when we don't spend regular time with Him? Of course. But none of that ever affects His love. His grace is free, and it never changes. Be a family that talks often about Jesus and that keeps going back to the Cross. That's where grace was purchased. That's where your kids need to be grounded, even when they fail. *Especially* when they fail.

You need to have a home that majors on the basics of salvation. It isn't about being religious and moral, about keeping all the rules, about going to church and reading the Bible and giving. Those things are great, but they have zero effect on God's love for us. The idea that God is weighing our good deeds and will allow us into heaven if the good outweighs the bad is heresy. Salvation is to be lived out in love for and gratitude to God, empowered by the Holy Spirit, and fed by the truth of God's Word. It's grace through faith in Christ every step of the way. That's the way we are saved, and that's the way we live out our salvation. That's the Christian life.

How can you know if your child is living a grace-filled life? Thanksgiving. Gratitude is always an accurate barometer of spiritual health. Children who believe they deserve everything they get (and more) do not understand grace. Those who understand grace aren't demanding and complaining. An attitude of thanksgiving is the clearest indication that the heart recognizes the unmerited love of God. To a heart like that, failure is never a surprise, and grace is always available.

LIVING OUT THE LESSON: TEACH YOUR CHILDREN THAT FAILURE IS NEVER FINAL

You can help your children understand that failure is never final by extending grace to those around you. You probably know people who lack integrity, who are living in sexual sin, who have stolen money, who are hypocritical, or who have a terrible temper. What attitude do you have toward those people? How do your kids see you respond to them? Ideally, they should understand that you have extremely high standards, but that you balance those standards with extreme grace toward everyone who doesn't meet them—including your kids and yourself. Every time I sensed real

An attitude of thanksgiving is the clearest indication that the heart recognizes the unmerited love of God.

brokenness in one of my children, I never felt that harsh discipline was necessary. Once they understood the standard they fell short of, it was time for grace.

If you treat people with the attitude that failure is never final, they'll know what it means to worship a God for whom our failure is never final. Your children should never fear getting written off by Mom or Dad, no matter what they've done and no matter how old they are. Living in an imperfect household, as you and I do, you'll have plenty of opportunities to express forgiveness. Grace doesn't compromise righteousness, but it should be extravagant enough to cover the worst of sins.

Make grace really practical in your home. First, make it a safe place by asking your children how you can help them when they've blown it. Don't solve their predicament; rather, give them all the room they need to own up to a failure without beating them over the head with it, take them by the hand to reconnect them with God and whomever else they've offended, and get them started on a new journey in another direction.

Second, show your child how to repent. The New Testament word for *repent* is *metanoia: meta* means "change," and *noia* means "mind." Repentance is a shifting of the mind. A repentant person mentally turns from what was wrong to what is right, both in attitude and action. It isn't simply sorrow for getting caught; it's a piercing of the heart that recognizes how God is grieved by sin.

I remember seeing tears streaming down my mother's face once after she spanked me. I didn't understand at first why she was crying more than me, but I realized that my disobedience was more than a rule violation. It was a relationship violation. That broke my heart, and I didn't want to hurt her anymore. It's the same way with God. Sin grieves Him, and it should break our hearts when we realize that we've violated the relationship. That changes our thinking and our behavior. That dynamic needs to be visible in your home.

Illustrate repentance for your children every time you blow it. Once our family was visiting my parents in Florida. My father was an ex-Marine, a pretty tough guy, and the thought of asking your kids to forgive you was a foreign concept to him. But I was trying hard to learn how to be a good dad while my kids were still small. I overreacted and yelled at my son Ryan for something he had done. Realizing my anger wasn't appropriate to the situation, I got down on one knee, looked my son in the eye, told him I was sorry, and asked him to forgive me. He said, "Sure, Dad," blew me a kiss, and went off to look for an alligator.

A couple of hours later, my father approached me. "I watched you with your son," he said. "What are you doing?"

"What do you mean, 'What are you doing?' "

"He's the kid, you're the parent. You don't need to apologize to him."

"Dad, I was wrong. He needs to know how someone should act when they're wrong."

That was a strange concept to my father, who didn't come to Christ until after he was fifty. But that's how kids learn. They watch us. So teach them to repent by doing it when you need to. Give them a clear message that every human being was created to receive grace and to give grace.

As parents, we all find ourselves in situations we never expected. We will look in the mirror one day in disbelief that the one we see could have failed so miserably. For some of you reading these words, failure may include years of neglect, outbursts of anger, spiritual negligence, or even abuse. But if you think that person in the mirror has made mistakes that are uncorrectable and that your children must live with the consequences the rest of their lives, you're wrong. Nothing could be further from the truth.

God wants you to know that no failure is final with Him. Just as Peter was completely forgiven and restored to usefulness after his willful betrayal of Jesus, God wants us to know that mercy triumphs over judgment. The most powerful way your child, regardless of age, will learn of the grace of God is by first seeing you receive grace from God and then extend grace to others.

When one of my sons was in high school, an image popped up on a computer and caught him by surprise. He wasn't looking for it, but there it was. That began a secret, several-months-long battle during which pictures on the Internet seduced his mind and heart. Because he was a passionate follower of Jesus, he began to live with extraordinary levels of guilt. He would read the Bible and pray, promising God he would never again look at pictures like that, only to find himself repeating the process twenty-four hours later.

In God's sovereign timing, I asked one of our information technology employees to stop by my house to look at my work computer. It was acting up and needed some adjustments. As he examined the hard drive, he confronted me with some honest questions about my viewing habits. I had no idea where these images came from, but I knew they weren't from me or my wife. I wrestled with the possibilities and implications, spending quite a bit of time in prayer about it. I confronted my son with the evidence and asked if he had been the user at these sites.

He immediately denied it, but within minutes was in tears,

confessing his struggle, his terrible guilt, and the turmoil he'd been living with for months. He told me how thankful he was that he had gotten caught and admitted that he needed help. I was hurt, of course, but the depth of his pain allowed me to feel God's heart, not for judgment, but for mercy. My son repented and began experiencing the truth that failure is never final. He took some drastic steps to remove himself from that temptation and has since shared his experience with other college and high school students with similar struggles. He both received grace and extended it to others.

I can't help but think our response as parents was crucial in my son's ability to grasp God's full forgiveness. We in no way undermined the concept of consequences—he experienced many, both as a natural result of his struggle and imposed by us in the process. But he learned that mercy really does triumph over judgment (James 2:13).

We and our children need to know at the very core of our hearts that failure is never final with Christ. Where sin abounds, grace superabounds. That's true for me, that's true for you, and that's true for every one of your children. With Jesus there is always hope, regardless of the depth of our failure.

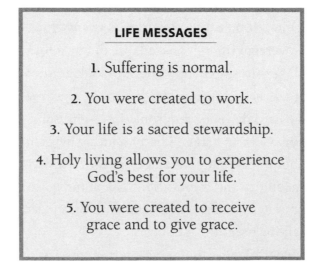

LIFE MESSAGES

1. Suffering is normal.

2. You were created to work.

3. Your life is a sacred stewardship.

4. Holy living allows you to experience God's best for your life.

5. You were created to receive grace and to give grace.

Putting It into Practice

Holiness is such an important concept for your children to grasp—and one they will never pick up from the culture in which we live. Without holiness, they will be ill-prepared to make wise decisions (see page 162).

Take some time to read together the following Scriptures that teach us about God's holiness. Discuss what they mean for us who follow Christ.

Exodus 3:5-6 _____

_____

Isaiah 6:1-8 _____

_____

1 Peter 1:15-16 _____

_____

Revelation 4:1-11 _____

_____

Though your children should understand that you have high standards, they also should realize that you balance those standards with extreme grace toward everyone who doesn't meet them—in other words, you should model that failure is never final. Consider the last time one of your children really blew it. Did you demonstrate grace to him or her? Is there anything you might do differently in the future?

_____

_____

_____

_____

Now that you've worked through this book, can you identify the one area in which you would most like to grow as a parent? As you look to

God to help, are you extending the same grace toward yourself as He does to you? Explain.

_____

_____

_____

_____

CONCLUSION

If you search the Bible for good parenting models, you're going to have a hard time finding them. The first parents, for example, raised a son who killed his brother. The patriarchs were about as dysfunctional as families can get: Abraham slept with his wife's servant—at his wife's suggestion!—to help God out with His plans, and the descendants of his first two sons have been at odds with each other ever since. Rebekah helped Jacob deceive his father for the firstborn's blessing; and Jacob clearly played favorites with his twelve sons, one of whom was sold into slavery by his brothers. The early heroes of our faith are not necessarily heroes of parenthood.

That trend continued. Samson's parents couldn't get a handle on his passions when he was young, so he couldn't get a handle on them when he was older. Eli gave his two sons mild verbal rebukes for their grievous sins as unrighteous priests, and the entire nation suffered. Even David, the man after God's own heart, the greatest king of Israel's history, didn't manage his family well. One of his sons raped a half-sister and received only a reprimand, and another son died in anger and bitterness in a failed coup d'état attempt against his father, David. No, if you're looking for the model parent in the Bible, you'll look a long time.

What's the point? The point is that God shows us in His inspired

Word that He has always been in the business of raising godly kids from imperfect parents. Families, as you well know, are a messy business, and the Bible never hides that fact. God could have filled His Word with all-star fathers and mothers, but He didn't. All-star mothers and fathers are hard to relate to. But even in the midst of tragic failures, God still accomplished His plan through godly young people who grew up to be godly adults. In spite of massive imperfections, grace was enough.

Remember that whenever you need to be encouraged. Hannah's offering of her son to God preserved godliness in a frequently rebellious nation. Solomon had a lot of good, timeless advice for his children, some of which I've quoted in this book. The faith of Timothy's mother was effectively passed down and preserved in her son, making him a treasured help to the great apostle Paul. The faith and obedience of Mary and Joseph were strong enough that God could entrust His only Son to their care. Among all the messiness, God chose people who had a heart for Him, and they and their children have changed the world.

Of course, the only perfect parenting example in the Bible—in the history of the world, for that matter—is God Himself. We've already talked about how He disciplines His children out of love, how He never compromises His holiness while also never withholding His grace. We've seen how Paul's firm yet tender words to his spiritual children exemplified both the maternal and paternal sides of God's love. We've gotten glimpses of the perfect Parent, and we've asked Him to help us with the hard task of raising our children.

Let me leave one last glimpse of that Father with you. It's found in Luke 15:11-32, and it's a great picture and a great reminder of the kind of parent we all strive to become. A young man with a selfish, rebellious streak asks his dad for his inheritance—long before dad is ready to die. The son squanders that inheritance on the vile, worthless idols of his heart. But in his desperation, this son returns to his father, hoping for enough mercy to work for hire.

There is much more mercy than that, as you recall. The father runs enthusiastically to his son and throws his arms around him, forgives him, restores him, and even welcomes him home with a party. The other son is outraged, but the father demonstrates his patient, generous heart toward him too. Neither son is perfect— not by a long shot—but neither son is written off—also not by a long shot. The father's standards never change, but his mercy and wisdom cover everything. His riches are given to two boys who need to learn how to use them wisely. And the father gives them ample opportunity to do that.

Have you considered that this wonderful father has two grown sons who still aren't very mature? Yes, I know—it's a parable, not a biography. But it's a parable that reveals the heart of God, and there's a reason this father is still busy teaching his kids when they're adults. It's because parenting is always messy and because kids always need loving, wise parents.

You'll need to remember that grace-filled story every time you feel as if you've blown it. You'll also need to reflect on it every time your child has blown it. And after repentance has occurred and mercy has been received, you'll need to adopt the attitude of the perfect father.

You see, even God's parenting is messy. Even His children rebel. It isn't because He doesn't know what He's doing; it's because He has ordained this world to be a learning process. His children eventually learn to walk, learn to be responsible, and learn to make wise decisions. They eventually develop the character of their Father. But they stumble a lot along the way, and God lets them. He is always patiently, lovingly, and firmly getting them back on their feet and pointing them in the right direction. He *never* gives up on His kids.

Neither should you. If you read this book and thought, *Sounds good, but it's too late for my kids*, you're wrong. It's never too late. One of the most powerful things parents can do is own up to their mistakes and dedicate themselves to parenting God's way. God has a way of getting a lot of mileage from feeble steps of obedience. Get in line with His will and let Him deal with the rest.

Your desires for your children are great. You would probably give them the world if you could. God understands that. His desires for your children are also great, and He has a wonderful purpose for them. But in your attempts to be a godly parent, remember God's great dreams for you too. Being a good parent is part of the package. He is intensely involved in the endeavor you're going through. Just as it's a learning process for your kids, it's a learning process for you. And God is with you every step of the way.

NOTES

1. See St. Neots Packaging Group information on kids meal promotions at http://www.fastfoodpackaging.com/promo.htm.
2. Lawrence Kohlberg, *The Philosophy of Moral Development: Essays on Moral Development*, vol. 1 (San Francisco: Harper and Row, 1981).
3. Gene Bedley, "Responsibility Means 'I Can Do Things on My Own,'" *Christian Parenting Today* (May/June 1990), 41.
4. B. O'Reilly, "Why Grade 'A' Execs Get an 'F' as Parents," *Fortune* (January 1, 1990), 36–46.
5. Reuben Hills's research as presented by Dr. Richard Meier in a seminar on parenting, MinirthMeier Clinic, Dallas, Texas, 1988.
6. Charles Swindoll explores the meaning of these two terms in depth in his book *You and Your Child* (Nashville: Thomas Nelson, 1977), 87–99.
7. James Dobson, *The New Strong-Willed Child* (Carol Stream, IL.: Tyndale, 2004), 65.
8. Margie Mason, "Study: Childhood Spanking Leaves No Permanent Scars," *Santa Cruz Sentinel* (August 25, 2001), A-1.
9. John L. Ronsvalle and Sylvia Ronsvalle, *The State of Church Giving Through 2000* (Champaign, IL: Empty Tomb, 2002).
10. American Academy of Child and Adolescent Psychiatry, "Facts for Families #54" (February 2005); http://www.aacap.org/publications/factsfam/tv.htm.

Free Discussion Guide!

A reproducible version of this
book's discussion questions is available at:

FOCUS ON THE FAMILY®

Welcome to the family!

Whether you purchased this book, borrowed it, or received it as a gift, we're glad you're reading it. It's just one of the many helpful, encouraging, and biblically based resources produced by Focus on the Family for people in all stages of life.

Focus began in 1977 with the vision of one man, Dr. James Dobson, a licensed psychologist and author of numerous best-selling books on marriage, parenting, and family. Alarmed by the societal, political, and economic pressures that were threatening the existence of the American family, Dr. Dobson founded Focus on the Family with one employee and a once-a-week radio broadcast aired on 36 stations.

Now an international organization reaching millions of people daily, Focus on the Family is dedicated to preserving values and strengthening and encouraging families through the life-changing message of Jesus Christ.

Focus on the Family Magazines

These faith-building, character-developing publications address the interests, issues, concerns, and challenges faced by every member of your family from preschool through the senior years.

| Focus on the Family **Citizen®** U.S. news issues | Focus on the Family **Clubhouse Jr.™** Ages 4 to 8 | Focus on the Family **Clubhouse™** Ages 8 to 12 | **Breakaway®** Teen guys | **Brio®** Teen girls 12 to 16 | **Brio & Beyond®** Teen girls 16 to 19 | **Plugged In®** Reviews movies, music, TV |

FOR MORE INFORMATION

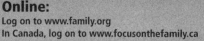

Online:
Log on to www.family.org
In Canada, log on to www.focusonthefamily.ca

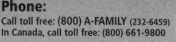

Phone:
Call toll free: (800) A-FAMILY (232-6459)
In Canada, call toll free: (800) 661-9800

BP06XFM

Now What?

===============

You've learned the basic principles of Effective Parenting but how do you apply them?

Go deeper and connect with others who are walking the same road with Walk Thru the Bible's *Effective Parenting in a Defective World* Small Group DVD Kit.

All it takes is a coffeepot, DVD player, and willing parents.

Start Now!
www.kidswhostandout.com
(800) 361-6131

===============

WALK THRU THE BIBLE®